Institute of International Studies

University of California

CHINESE DYNASTIC HISTORIES TRANSLATIONS
No. 9

BIOGRAPHY OF YÜ-WEN HU

Translated and Annotated
By ALBERT E. DIEN

UNIVERSITY OF CALIFORNIA PRESS
Berkeley and Los Angeles · 1962

Chinese Dynastic Histories Translations: No. 9

Editors: S. H. Chen, Woodbridge Bingham, Wolfram Eberhard,
H. H. Frankel, C. S. Goodrich, Elizabeth Huff,
O. J. Maenchen, M. C. Rogers
Assistant Editor: R. J. Krompart

University of California Press, Berkeley and Los Angeles
Cambridge University Press, London, England

© 1962 by The Regents of the University of California

Preface

The translation of the biography of Yü-wen Hu was done originally under the guidance of Professor Peter A. Boodberg, and formed my thesis for the Master of Art's degree. During the process of editing for appearance in this series, many suggestions for improvement were made by Professors Ch'en Shih-hsiang and Hans Frankel, Dr. Chauncey Goodrich, Mr. Robert Krompart, and others, all of whom have devoted much time and effort to it. The faults which still remain are clear testimony to the rudimentary nature of the original manuscript. I can only offer my inadequate apologies to all those named above, and credit them with any merit the present work may possess.

Honolulu A. E. Dien
June 30, 1962

Contents

Introduction 1
Notes to Introduction 24
Translation (Chou shu 11.1a-17b, 22b-23b) 30
Notes to Translation 64
Bibliography of Principal Works Cited and Used 116
Chinese Text (Chou shu 11.1a-17b, 22b-23b) 123
Index 159
Map . . . . In pocket
Genealogical Chart of Yü-wen Family . . . . In pocket

Abbreviations

BMFEA	Bulletin of the Museum of Far Eastern Antiquities (Stockholm)
BSOAS	Bulletin of the School of Oriental and African Studies (London)
CS	Chou shu 周書
HJAS	Harvard Journal of Asiatic Studies
NS	Nan shih 南史
PCS	Pei-Ch'i shu 北齊書
PS	Pei shih 北史
TCTC	Tzu-chih t'ung-chien 資治通鑑
TP	T'oung Pao
TSFYCY	Tu-shih fang-yü chi-yao 讀史方輿紀要
TT	T'ung-tien 通典
SPTK	Ssu-pu ts'ung-k'an 四部叢刊
WS	Wei shu 魏書

Unless otherwise indicated, the Chinese dynastic histories are translated and cited from the edition in Po-na pen erh-shih-ssu shih 百衲本二十四史 (Shanghai: Commercial Press, 1930-37) and classical citations are to Sung-pen Shih-san-ching chu-su fu chiao-k'an-chi 宋本十三經注疏附校勘記, Juan Yüan 阮元 ed., Wood block ed., 1826.

Introduction

There have been in recent years a number of publications dealing with northern China between the fall of the Han and the establishment of the T'ang; intellectual, social, and political trends have been pointed out and discussed, and some attempt has been made to assay the value of the contributions of the northern states to the history of China as a whole. Much specialized work remains, nevertheless, before a true synthetic history of the period can be undertaken.

In the West, "exaggerated interest in the picturesque figures of history" has been thoroughly (and properly) discredited as a viable analytic approach to the past, and in sinological studies, as well, works characterized by such an emphasis are of only the most limited value. On the other hand, because of the well-known difficulties of research in oriental languages, serious biographical studies arranged for handy reference have a greater value to sinologists than they do to specialists in other fields. When, in addition, such a biographical study is executed as a faithful translation of a Chinese document that preserves contemporary modes of expression and thought, embodies concrete sociological and intellectual problems of culture-transition (such as those involved in the establishment and preservation of a Confucian state by a group not yet very far removed from alien origins) and presents in detail moral conflicts of great abstract and practical significance, it is clearly of use to the sinologist and to the student of comparative culture.

Such a position among the documents pertaining to the politics of northern China in the sixth century is held by the Chou shu biography of Yü-wen Hu 宇文護 (513?-572),[1] who lived in the area controlled first by the Northern (T'o-pa) Wei, later by the Western Wei, and then by the Northern Chou. His biography presents us with an example of one way in which rulers of foreign derivation in the north modeled their policies (at least those recorded by the historian) on traditional patterns of Confucian China and used and adapted Chinese moral norms in their struggles with political exigency.

Rarely in reading the biography is one made aware by the historian that the Yü-wen rulers and the majority of their followers were of non-Chinese origin. Perhaps this characteristic of the presentation, which marks the Chou shu as a whole, derived from the effective implementation of Confucian social modes in most areas of life and, therefore, from the subjects' being already so sinified that they were no longer considered alien. Perhaps it merely follows naturally from the historian's using as source material state documents cast in purely Confucian terms. Or perhaps the historian was unable (or unwilling) to adapt traditional historiographic forms to reveal non-Chinese influence in the history of the Northern Chou.

The early ancestors of the Yü-wen[2] are described in Chinese sources as distant vassals of the southern Hsiung-nu confederation, and they are first referred to as the leading clan of the tribes of eastern Manchuria.[3] At the end of the third century of our era the Yü-wen migrated into southern Manchuria,[4] where they became quite important for a short time, but in the fourth century they came into conflict with the Mu-jung 慕容, who were in the process of establishing their Yen 燕 state (341-370). The last of the independent Yü-wen rulers, I-tou-kuei 逸豆歸,[5] was decisively defeated by Mu-jung Huang 慕容晃, and in 344 Huang invaded their lands. I-tou-kuei fled to northern Korea, while his tribesmen were transported south to Ch'ang-li 昌黎, north of modern Pei-p'ing.[6]

Their defeat by the Mu-jung marked the start of a new stage in the history of the Yü-wen family. I-tou-kuei's son Ling 陵 first served the Yen state and was enfeoffed as Duke of Hsüan-t'u 玄菟. When Yen fell, Yü-wen Ling shifted his allegiance to the ascendant T'o-pa Wei, and at the turn of the fifth century he moved his family to Wu-ch'uan 武川.[7] The Yü-wen family of the Northern Chou traced their ancestry directly to Ling, during and after whose lifetime the Yü-wen, far from being the powerful tribal leaders of old, seem to have become merely well-to-do tribesmen of moderate influence.

Yü-wen Hu grew up in a period of growing unrest in north China and of increasing weakness in the Wei court at Lo-yang.[8] In 524 P'o-liu-han Pa-ling 破六汗拔陵 raised the standard of revolt at Wo-yeh Garrison 沃野鎮. The Yü-wen, led by Hu's grandfather Hung 肱, gathered with other leading families of the area to come to the defense of the court and killed the rebels' prince, Wei K'o-ku 衛可孤,[9] but a large group of K'o-ku's followers soon overtook Hung, and in the subsequent skirmish Hung's son Hao 顥 (Yü-wen Hu's father) was killed. Because of the precarious situation, Hung decided to lead his family southwards, but en route the family, including Hao's three sons, Shih-fei 什肥, Tao 導, and Hu, fell into the hands of another of the semi-independent chieftains of the region, Hsien-yü Hsiu-li 鮮于修禮, who ordered Hung to return to his home and resume control of his lands. This was to be accomplished, presumably, with Hsiu-li's military support.[10] Pa-ling continued his expansion, but in the next year, 525, he was attacked and defeated by the Juan-juan and was immediately succeeded by another rebel, Tu Lo-chou 杜洛周.[11]

Early in 526 Hsien-yü Hsiu-li decided to declare open rebellion. He established his own reign-title, and in due course troops were sent from the capital against him. He had some success at first and forced those troops to withdraw.[12] Since the Yü-wen family was involved in the rebellion through its bond with Hsiu-li, Yü-wen Hung again decided to move his family to greater safety. On the way an imperial army attacked and killed Hung and his son Lien. The wives of Hung's three sons, each with a child, were taken captive, but with the aid of Hsiu-li[13] they soon effected their release. Shortly after, Hsiu-li was killed, and Ko Jung 葛榮, who may have been a subordinate of Hsiu-li, took over the leadership of the army.[14] The remaining sons of Hung, that is, Lo-sheng and T'ai, became officers in the army of Ko Jung, who, after defeating some government troops, named himself the emperor of a new dynasty, the (Northern) Ch'i 齊, and soon began to expand his territory. Because of the activities of Tu Lo-chou to the north, he turned his attention to the south, where he came into conflict with another military leader, Erh-chu Jung 爾朱榮.

The Erh-chu family had long been recognized as the military chieftains of the Hsiu-jung 秀榮 area in central Shansi. As the Wei weakened, they had grown in power but had never thrown off their nominal allegiance to the emperor.[15] Now, however, the court at Lo-yang had all but collapsed, and Erh-chu Jung was being urged by some of his followers to take over the government. At first he hesitated. Then, early in 528, spurred on by a letter from the emperor, he marched on the capital and put a new prince on the throne.[16] Erh-chu Jung then turned his attention once again to Ko Jung. Throughout 527 and the beginning of 528 Ko Jung had been advancing to the south. By combining forces with Tu Lo-chou, he had been able to raid as far south as the Ch'in 沁 River in southern Shansi.[17] Despite this apparent success, however, Yü-wen T'ai is said to have realized the futility of Ko Jung's efforts to win over the whole country; he therefore prepared to flee with his brothers and nephews, but before this could be done, the armies of Ko Jung and Erh-chu Jung met, and Ko Jung and his army were captured. Lo-sheng was killed because his bravery and martial ardor made him a dangerous enemy, but T'ai saved his own life by a stirring appeal. Erh-chu Jung not only spared his life but also appointed him to a military office.[18]

During its brief tenure of power (528-532) the Erh-chu clan was continually obliged to defend its own position and the boundaries of the state by force of arms. In 530 Erh-chu Jung sent an army into Shensi to put down a threatening revolt. Ho-pa Yüeh was put in actual charge of the army, and Yü-wen T'ai was assigned to it. Yüeh had long been associated with T'ai's family and is even said to have shot the arrow that killed Wei K'o-ku six years before. The campaign was successful despite the procrastination of its nominal head, Erh-chu T'ien-kuang 爾朱天光, and the western part of the state seemed secure.[19]

For his part in the victory T'ai became a prefect.

But even while its armies were stabilizing the west, the Erh-chu clan fell to internecine quarreling in 530. By 532 Kao Huan 高歡, one of its generals, was able to destroy the whole family and become <u>de facto</u> ruler of the empire. When Erh-chu T'ien-kuang had left Shensi in 531 to aid in the struggle against Kao Huan, Ho-pa Yüeh and another general, Hou-mo-ch'en Yüeh 侯莫陳悅, had taken advantage of the opportunity and captured Ch'ang-an, helping to bring about the downfall of the Erh-chu.[20] Kao Huan naturally expected the armies in the west to transfer their allegiance to him, but at the urging of Yü-wen T'ai Ho-pa Yüeh refrained from submitting to Kao Huan and instead offered his support to the puppet emperor at Lo-yang. In 534, while campaigning to bring all of the territory west of the T'ung Pass 潼關 under his sway, Ho-pa Yüeh was treacherously slain by Hou-mo-ch'en Yüeh, who had made overtures to Kao Huan.[21] The assassin attempted to assume the leadership of the area, but the armies of Ho-pa Yüeh, led by Yü-wen T'ai, continued the policies of their former general. Receiving the sanction of the court, T'ai defeated Hou-mo-ch'en Yüeh and his allies.[22]

Thus Yü-wen T'ai and his armies in the west found themselves in a peculiar position: they were placing themselves nominally under an emperor who was apparently friendly to their enemy, Kao Huan. Kao Huan, for his part, realized the dangers which this situation posed for his own regime and decided to put the Emperor under closer surveillance. He marched on Lo-yang, but Yü-wen T'ai forestalled him by having the Emperor brought into Shensi, or, as the <u>Chou shu</u> has it, "enter the pass" (ju kuan 入關).²³ Kao Huan immediately established another T'o-pa prince as emperor, and the definitive division of the Wei state was thus completed.

Neither Kao Huan, de facto master of the Eastern Wei, nor Yü-wen T'ai, in control of Western Wei, expected the partition to remain, since it seemed to be just one of the many conflicts between military leaders which always ended in the triumph of one side. The next few years were taken up with the attempts of each to conquer the other. The campaigns were inconclusive, but Eastern Wei, at first the aggressor, was gradually put on the defensive. In 537 Tou T'ai entered T'ung Pass as leader of one element of a three-pronged attack on Western Wei. He was attacked by Yü-wen T'ai before he could form his lines, his army was captured, and he committed suicide. As Yü-wen T'ai had predicted, the news of the defeat caused the other Eastern Wei columns to withdraw.²⁴

Later the same year Yü-wen T'ai led an army eastward as far as Hung-nung 弘農. He was initially successful, but he finally had to withdraw because his troops were outnumbered. Kao Huan attempted to press his advantage and followed the retreating army through T'ung Pass. They fought at Sha-yüan 沙苑, and Huan was defeated by superior tactics. Tu-ku Hsin 獨孤信, one of T'ai's generals, was then able to occupy Lo-yang. The next year (538) Hsin was besieged. T'ai led some troops to his aid and suffered a defeat at Ho-ch'iao 河橋, north of the city,²⁵ but the area east of the T'ung Pass up to Hung-nung remained under the control of Western Wei. For the next few years there were only border skirmishes as Eastern Wei attempted to halt the slow encroachment of the Western Wei on its territory.

In the beginning of 543 T'ai led another army toward Lo-yang. Kao Huan and his forces arrived north of the Yellow River and shortly afterwards managed to cross it. Huan established his battle lines on the Mang Hills 邙山, just north of Lo-yang, and remained there for several days. T'ai then led his men up the mountain at night and on May 8 joined in battle. T'ai, on the right flank, was successful and purportedly captured many of the enemy, but on the left flank Chao Kuei 趙貴 and the other generals were defeated and driven back. This forced T'ai himself to withdraw, and the battle was lost with the sacrifice of many men. T'ai led the army in retreat back through T'ung Pass, but an effort on the part of Kao Huan to follow up the victory was repulsed.

On his return T'ai asked to be dismissed because of the defeat. The emperor naturally refused, but Chao Kuei and other generals and officers, including Yü-wen Hu, were removed from office, although later all were returned to their posts.[26]

The conflict between the two northern Chinese states also involved the southern state of Liang 梁. Its ruler Hsiao I was on good terms with Northern Ch'i, which succeeded Eastern Wei in 550, but relations were unfriendly between Liang and Western Wei. Small-scale armed clashes combined with T'ai's support of Hsiao Ch'a 蕭詧, a refractory prince of the Liang,[27] made for hostility in their relationship, and the ambitions of T'ai increased the tension.[28] Finally T'ai decided to invade Liang. One of the reasons given for the invasion was that an envoy of T'ai had been slighted at the Liang court on an occasion when an envoy of Ch'i was given preferential treatment.[29] In 554 Yü

Chin 于謹 was sent south with a force which included Yü-wen Hu, Yang Chung 楊忠, Wei Hsiao-k'uan 韋孝寬, and allegedly 500,000 troops.[30] When the armies crossed the Han River, Hu and Yang Chung led picked cavalry to capture a ford on the Yangtze and cut off the escape of the Liang troops. When Chin arrived, the Liang capital, Chiang-ling 江陵, was invested. It fell early in 555, and Hsiao I was killed. Hsiao Ch'a was made puppet ruler at Chiang-ling, while the Liang itself continued its existence at Tan-yang 丹陽 under a son of the late emperor.[31] This was the last large-scale campaign during the Western Wei period.

It may now be asked how secure was Yü-wen T'ai's position as de facto ruler of the Western Wei, a position based initially on a small group of devoted followers whom T'ai placed in key military and civil positions. The annals of the Chou shu list the names of twelve generals led by him in the campaign of Hung-nung in 537.[32] These twelve and some others remained the core of his military staff. Nine of the twelve, including Li Pi 李弼, Chao Kuei, and Hou-mo-ch'en Ch'ung, entered Shensi in the armies of Ho-pa Yüeh and Erh-chu T'ien-kuang. Yü Chin and Li Yüan 李遠 had joined the Western Wei forces later. Tu-ku Hsin had been sent by Ho-pa Yüeh's brother Sheng 勝 to help control the situation that resulted from Yüeh's death. Of the ten generals from "beyond the passes," eight were from the area of Wu-ch'uan, the home of the Yü-wen family. All ten had served in the armies of Ko Jung, Erh-chu Jung, or both.

Yü-wen T'ai brought these men into controlling positions in the new organizational system which he introduced into the army in the late 530's. T'ai himself and seven others were appointed Pillar of State Great Generals (chu-kuo ta-chiang-chün 柱國大將軍). T'ai was supreme commander of military affairs, another of the eight directed the imperial bodyguard, and the remaining six were in command of the armies. Attached to each of these six were two Great Generals, each of whom was in charge of two Palatines (k'ai-fu 開府), who, in turn, each directed an army. Thus there were twenty-four armies in all.[33] The list of eight Pillar of State Great Generals and twelve Great Generals reveals the same close-knit structure. Of the former rank, the only newcomers were Yüan Hsin 元欣, a T'o-pa prince, and Li Hu 李虎, also a native of Wu-ch'uan, who, incidentally, was the grandfather of the first emperor of the T'ang. Among the twelve Great Generals, two had been included in the list of twelve generals in 537, and the remainder numbered three T'o-pa princes, a nephew, a cousin, a more distant relative of T'ai, and two men from Wu-ch'uan. One of the latter was Yang Chung, the father of the founder of the Sui dynasty. Yü-wen T'ai is said to have treated his close associates as equals. They played an important part in official discussions and were, to a man, loyal to T'ai.

When T'ai instituted his governmental organization based on the Chou li in 556,[34] the same men were given important posts of government. In 556, just before T'ai's death, the heads of the bureaus were:

Yü-wen T'ai	Great Chancellor (ta chung-tsai 大冢宰)
Li Pi	Minister of Education (ta ssu-t'u 大司徒)
Chao Kuei	Minister of Rites (ta tsung-po 大宗伯)
Tu-ku Hsin	Grand Constable (ta ssu-ma 大司馬)

Yü Chin	Minister of Crime (ta ssu-k'ou 大司寇)
Hou-mo-ch'en Ch'ung	Minister of Public Works (ta ssu-k'ung 大司空)

Despite the loyalty of his followers, T'ai must have felt apprehensive about the future. He was merely the chancellor of the state, and, his influence being of a personal nature, there was no guarantee of familial succession. On the other hand, there was ample precedent for the son of the de facto ruler of a state to inaugurate a new dynasty on the death of his father. With T'ai's son declared emperor, the fortunes of the family would be ensured.

The inauguration of a new dynasty, however, was a precarious business requiring the exercise of extraordinary care and judgment, an undertaking the guidance of which T'ai could ill afford to entrust either to his sons, who were too young, or to anyone outside his family. He therefore turned to his nephew Hu, the eldest member of his immediate family.[35]

In 556 Hu was still relatively unimportant. He had taken an increasingly greater part in the military campaigns, especially against Liang in 554, and had acquitted himself well. In 556, when he was appointed Assistant Minister of Public Works, he still ranked below such veterans as Chao Kuei and Tu-ku Hsin, but when T'ai was on his deathbed, he summoned Hu and entrusted to him the responsibility for the family fortunes and the guardianship of T'ai's son and heir Chüeh.

Yü-wen Hu was thus suddenly faced with the difficult task of maintaining the supremacy of the Yü-wen family when its strong leader, Yü-wen T'ai, was no longer alive and when T'ai's son Chüeh, who inherited from his father the offices of Grand Tutor and Chancellor, was only fourteen years old. The influential nobles could be expected to exert every effort to increase their own spheres of control, a development which, if allowed to proceed, would eventually make the young heir's position as void of real power as the ruling Wei emperor's had become. Yü-wen Hu could succeed only if he managed to use the loyalty of the followers of the dead Yü-wen T'ai to strengthen the position of T'ai's son Chüeh and, indirectly, to consolidate his own position as Chüeh's guardian.

The implementation of T'ai's last wishes was to be discussed by the nobles at a court meeting. Before the meeting Yü-wen Hu turned to Yü Chin, a close and devoted follower of T'ai, for advice. Yü Chin urged Hu to show no reticence in pressing his claims and at the meeting personally made a speech that recalled how T'ai had restored order and made the state strong. He then exhorted the assemblage to continue their good fortune by swearing fealty to T'ai's heir Chüeh and to Chüeh's guardian Hu. At this point Hu said he could not refuse the responsibility which had been thrust upon him. Yü Chin and then the other nobles, perhaps carried away by Yü Chin's emotional appeal and the desire to maintain unity, rushed to pledge their allegiance to Hu.[36]

Although the controlling position of the Yü-wen family had been preserved, it still rested on an uncertain basis. To stabilize the situation and complete Yü-wen T'ai's plan, it was necessary to replace the Wei emperor with T'ai's heir. In this way the pattern of the imperial state, with its institutionalized respect and loyalty, could strengthen the security of the family and provide regular lines of succession. The nobles themselves probably envisioned a change of dynasty when they pledged their allegiance to Yü-wen Chüeh and Hu.

When the Northern Chou was inaugurated with Yü-wen Chüeh as emperor and Hu as regent, one of the most influential figures at the court, Chao Kuei, carried the imperial seal to the new emperor, which may be taken to mean that he and the other generals approved of the change. But the tensions at the court were by no means lessened. From subsequent events it would seem that Yü-wen Hu believed T'ai's charge gave him the sanction to rule the state. The powerful nobles may have been willing to support Yü-wen Chüeh as emperor, but the growing power of Hu caused them concern. They perhaps felt that with the new emperor safely installed, the role of Hu as regent had become unnecessary, and naturally they desired to maintain and extend their influence, while Hu, on the other hand, felt certain that the interests of his family could be defended only by himself. It was inevitable that they should clash, and, in the show of force, Hu was victorious.

Although some of the nobles, such as Yü Chin and Li Pi, decided to support Hu, the most eminent, Chao Kuei and Tu-ku Hsin, were opposed to him, and the uneasy alliance that resulted from this situation was not broken until the discovery of a plot by Chao Kuei and Tu-ku Hsin to remove Hu. It was alleged that Chao Kuei had urged immediate action but that Tu-ku Hsin had persuaded him to delay. The plot was declared an act hostile to the state itself, and the two nobles, with their followers, were executed. Hu then became chancellor of the state, the position formerly held by Chao Kuei.

Hu was now firmly in control. He strengthened his position by giving the important offices to men more amenable to him than had been the proud, independent veterans associated with T'ai. Li Pi died in 557, and Hou-mo-ch'en Ch'ung was forced to commit suicide in 563. In place of those officials, Hu brought into the cabinet his cousins, Yü-ch'ih Kang 尉遲綱 and Ho-lan Hsiang 賀蘭祥, and old generals such as Ta-hsi Wu 達奚武 and Tou-lu Ning 豆盧寧. The last two found no difficulty in changing their allegiance to Hu, since under T'ai they had not had the high status enjoyed by Chao Kuei and others. When Yang Chung was suggested as a possibility for filling one of the cabinet posts, Hu blocked the appointment, considering him to be too independent.

These bold moves by no means eliminated the opposition to Yü-wen Hu. Many were still disturbed by his control of the government. For example, Ch'i Kuei 齊軌 confided to an associate his opinion that the affairs of state should be administered by the emperor, not by a powerful minister, and he was executed when the statement was reported to Hu. Later in the year a plot more serious than that of Chao Kuei was uncovered, with the emperor himself a party to the conspiracy. To meet this crisis Hu had to abandon his role of protector of the emperor's personal safety. He turned to his relatives Ho-lan Hsiang, Yü-ch'ih Kang, and others and convinced them that in order to protect their own status they must remove the emperor himself. In the court discussion of this move, after the event, the courtiers are reported to have said: "This is an affair of your family. We dare not but hearken to your commands." Whether or not the courtiers actually used that classical phrase, the lack of any overt opposition contrasts sharply with the uncertain situation Yü-wen Hu had faced in the court a scant year before.

Hu acted with great acumen and decision in the critical early years of the Northern Chou dynasty, and he was credited with the establishment of the dynasty. The lack of any established tradition, the power of the generals, the extremely uncertain conditions in the country and in its relationships with other states, convinced Hu of the necessity for quick and firm action.[37] He gathered the reins of government into his hands and prevented any organized resistance to the new regime, seemingly convinced that the continued success of the new dynasty was entirely dependent upon him. To what degree a motive of self interest entered into his reasoning cannot be known, but it is clear that he felt himself to be indispensable.[38] When the first emperor appeared dissatisfied and the second showed signs of incipient independence, Hu had them removed. The third son of T'ai to occupy the throne was able to avoid any suspicion of disloyalty until there came an opportunity to murder Hu.

Since the early years of Hu's regency were devoted to stabilizing internal affairs, little action was taken against external enemies. There were a few punitive expeditions against the T'u-yü-hun and the Man tribes, and the T'u-chüeh were enticed into attacking Ch'i.[39] Neither the raids of the T'u-chüeh nor the one large-scale expedition by Chou forces against Ch'i were completely successful. In 563 and 564 Yang Chung made two raids with fair results, and in the latter year a full-scale attack on Ch'i was begun.

The invasion was perhaps foredoomed because Hu had no genuine desire to engage in a military campaign. The overall strategy was to have a four-pronged attack, the main advance to be made through T'ung Pass past Hung-nung to capture Lo-yang. Yang Piao 楊樞 was to go eastwards on the north side of the T'ai-hang Mountains 太行山 until he reached Chih Pass 軹關. He was then perhaps to turn south on Lo-yang, but it seems more probable that he was to secure the pass for the main army, which would turn north after the capture of Lo-yang to advance on Yeh 鄴, the Ch'i capital. Ch'üan Ching-hsüan 權景宣 was to take the southern route and neutralize the area south of Lo-yang. The fourth route was assigned to Yang Chung, the hero of the previous campaigns, who again was to lead the T'u-chüeh down from the north, but he met with opposition in his recruitment of men and supplies. By the time he had overcome the reluctance of some of the border tribes and had raised an army, the campaign was over.

The Ch'i forces appeared unexpectedly at Lo-yang. They found Yü-ch'ih Chiung directing the siege, but many of the Chou forces were north of the city, near the Mang Hills. Chiung's forces melted away, and only his acts of personal daring prevented a catastrophe. Ta-hsi Wu and Prince Hsien 憲王, at the head of the main advance army, were able to collect their troops and retreat safely. The only successful invasion column was the one led by Ch'üan Ching-hsüan. He penetrated the area south of the Yellow River and sent back to Ch'ang-an one thousand prisoners. But when the siege of Lo-yang was abandoned by the Chou troops, he collected his men and returned.

Disaster was incurred by Yang Piao. He had served on the

borders of Chou for over twenty years and, since in all that time he had not lost a battle, tended to belittle the quality of the Ch'i armies. He penetrated deeply into Ch'i territory, apparently without thought of danger, and then suddenly was surrounded and forced to surrender. But because of his extraordinary achievements in the past, the Chou court did not consider his surrender a crime, and his family therefore was not slaughtered or imprisoned.

Later military activities were hardly more successful. In 567 bitter fighting broke out with Ch'en, the state to the south, when an officer of Ch'en surrendered to Chou. Chou lost many men, and the territory to the south of the Yangtze fell to Ch'en.

Yü-wen Hu's name is not mentioned in any of the accounts of the Ch'i campaign, and it is probable that he did not go beyond Hung-nung. He was forced into the invasion of Ch'i because of promises made to the T'u-chüeh, and he had little to do with starting the war with Ch'en. It is probable that Hu had no interest in carrying on military campaigns. The decree issued after his death complained that "warriors relied on the strength of impeding walls." Because his position as regent was a precarious one, any disturbances were likely to affect him adversely, so diplomatic relations were quickly re-established with Ch'i, and in 569 the Northern Chou court was closed in observance of the death of a ruler of that state.

One of the most interesting features of the Northern Chou dynasty was its emulation of the ancient Chou. Yü-wen T'ai appears to have been deeply concerned with the moral fiber of his state. To strengthen it he attempted to discard what he felt was the decadent heritage of the Han-Wei period and fostered a return to the traditions of the Chou,[40] a program he carried to the point of organizing the government on the pattern found in the Chou li and styling official documents after the Shu ching. By the time of T'ai's death in 556, the foundation had been laid for a state modeled after the ancient Chou, a circumstance that made the figure of the Duke of Chou loom large in the thoughts of Yü-wen Hu.

The source of the legend of the Duke of Chou is the Shu ching. King Wu of the Chou state overthrew the evil last ruler of the Shang dynasty and established the Chou line. King Wu ruled for seven years and was succeeded at his death by his son Ch'eng. Because King Ch'eng, however, was only thirteen years of age, King Wu's brother Tan, the Duke of Chou, became regent. He held this post for seven years, retired, and died a few years later.

Thirteen of the books of the Shu ching deal with the words and actions of the Duke. These are concerned with the establishment of a new city, the organization of the government, and moralistic pronouncements, the most important of which are concerned with good government. Here are discussed the ideal of perfect government as well as the roles of ruler and officials and the duties of the people in bringing about the realization of the ideal.

The Duke of Chou often mentions the virtues of the past rulers and asks that they be taken as models. He speaks of the favor of Heaven and his wish that men act so as to merit it. The cumulative effect of all these statements and the strong endorsement of Confucius produce the image of a sage who constantly stresses the highest ideals of Chinese traditional society. A leading translator has written, "The Duke of Chou was undoubtedly one of the greatest men whom China has produced, and I do not know of any nation with whom his countrymen need shrink from comparing him." In this statement Legge was reflecting the traditional Chinese veneration of the Duke of Chou. However, during the Duke's lifetime he was not universally admired. From the well-known episode contained in the section Chin t'eng 金縢 ("The Metal-bound Coffer") of the Shu ching, we know that some of the Duke's brothers suspected him of designs on the throne and that the King for whom he was regent shared these suspicions. K'ung Ying-ta points out in his commentary on the Shu ching that these views were prompted by the practice of fraternal succession in the previous dynasty and by the fear that the Duke would use this precedent and his great power to seize the throne.[41] Even after the Duke of Chou had defeated his dissident brothers in a long campaign, the King persisted in his suspicions and eventually dismissed the Duke from his offices. The dismissal was achieved without difficulty, for the Duke had voluntarily abdicated his position as regent when the King came of age. Only years later, so runs the account, was the Duke vindicated by the discovery of a prayer in which he offered his own life to the gods in return for that of King Wu, who had fallen ill. The Duke of Chou's placing the welfare of the state above his own interests is an important element in the tradition of the Duke's saintliness.

As we have seen, Yü-wen Hu found himself in a very similar situation. He was the regent of a young emperor, the government was in his hands, and he was open to the suspicion of wanting to usurp the throne for himself. Filial succession was not the established pattern that it was in other, more settled, periods. Further, the position of regent was a logical contradiction in terms. The emperor proposed, the chancellor disposed; but during a regency, the regent as chancellor had, in addition, to assume powers which were imperial prerogatives. In such a case, the guidance was to be sought in the conduct of certain other regents in the past, notably the Duke of Chou and Ho Kuang of the Han. Thus these figures of the past were not mere precedents; they were rather archetypes by which one's own actions and attitudes could be formulated.

The removal of Tu-ku Hsin, the father-in-law of the emperor's eldest brother, and of Chao Kuei might be compared to the extermination of the Duke of Chou's brothers, who had threatened the welfare of the state. In the edict disclosing this plot, the emperor spoke of his youth and immaturity and his dependence on Hu. King Ch'eng was supposed to have spoken in the same vein when the Duke of Chou started on the campaign against his brothers.

That Hu very consciously attempted to emulate the Duke of Chou is revealed in the words of some men who were attempting to persuade the emperor to dispose of Hu. They said, "The Duke of Chin [Hu] frequently says, 'I now flank and support the throne. I desire to conduct affairs as did the Duke of Chou.' We your servants have heard that the Duke of Chou controlled the regency government for seven years. Only after this did he 'restore [the management of affairs] to the child, his intelligent prince.' How will Your Majesty endure [this state of affairs] as it is today for seven years?"[42]

Later, when Hu broke up the plot by sending the ringleaders to the provinces, the emperor wished to recall them, but Hu said to him: "The reason your servant has hustled and bustled and thus has interfered with your heaven-endowed majestic influence is only so that he might not fail T'ai-tsu's testamentary trust to protect and keep safe the good fortune of the state."[43] By emphasizing his concern for the welfare of the state, Hu could apply the principles of the Duke of Chou, strengthen his own position, and gain for his role the sanction of tradition.

In 561 an edict was promulgated which said in part: "As the virtue of the Duke of Chou was very great, Lu set up King Wen's ancestral temple. We consider Hu's achievements to be comparable to those of the Duke of Chou, and it is proper to use this ritual."[44] In the case of the Duke of Chou, it was after the discovery of the prayer in the metal-bound coffer that the privilege of the imperial sacrifices to heaven and the erection of the ancestral temple were granted to Lu, the Duke's fief. In this case Hu was given the right to build a separate ancestral temple dedicated to Yü-wen Hung and to sacrifice in it. We may suppose that this occasion was to mark the vindication of Hu, just as its prototype had served for the Duke of Chou.

Yü-wen Hu, unlike the Duke of Chou, did not give up his position as de facto ruler. He must have realized that this step could not be taken in the face of the ill will he had engendered. It was thus a fitting end to his role of emulating the Duke of Chou that he was killed while reading to the tippling Dowager Empress the Duke's words on the evils of liquor.

The Chou shu contains little praise of the period of Yü-wen Hu's regency. The picture given is one of harshness and favoritism. Hou-mo-ch'en Ch'ung was put to death merely for remarking aloud that Yü-wen Hu had died.[45] Yü-wen Hsien feared a break between the emperor and Hu and was always maneuvering to prevent it.[46] The common people were reduced to despair. In addition to this atmosphere of fear and repression, there was dissatisfaction with widespread graft and with the luxury in which Hu's favorites and children lived.[47] The charges are repeated in the decree issued after Hu's death, in which all of his faults are described. Much of the criticism may stem from disapproval of Yü-wen Hu's failure to observe the proper rules of relationship between ruler and subject.[48] In the decree the two elements, Hu's lack of virtue and the evil conditions in the state, are interrelated, the former conceived as generating the latter.

Since Yü-wen T'ai was held to have played the role of King Wu, the founder of the ancient Chou dynasty, and Hu to have emulated the Duke of Chou, it is in these two roles that the idealized contrast of their contribution is most readily seen. Under T'ai there had come into being a dynamic and powerful state with a moral and intellectual system that took its inspiration from the traditions of the Chou. On the other hand, while Hu had ensured the continuation of the dynasty, he had failed to live up to the standards of his model. The vigor that T'ai infused into the dynasty was soon exhausted, and no new developments were made. On the contrary, territory was lost and the desire for expansion died. The moral reorganization of the government begun under T'ai was replaced with harshness and corruption in Hu's period. It was only after the death of Hu that the state again regained some of its vitality.

The underlying assumptions of traditional literati historiography in China suffuse all documentary remains with a subtle and for the most part uncritical "praise and blame" exegesis, so moral and social forms sometimes have seemed in Chinese history to destroy individuality. But the inherent bias of evidence is, after all, a part of the data of history, and it is worthwhile to remember that tradition in China, as elsewhere, operated through conscious human will as well as through impersonal institutional patterns.

The idealized Confucian figure of the Duke of Chou provided Yü-wen Hu--and many others throughout Chinese history--with a paradigm, but only Hu's own volition could give the paradigm actuality in the politics of Northern Chou, a state that was founded, if one is to accept the argument of a great modern Chinese historian, on radically anti-Confucian principles of social structure.[49] And although the detailed description of the clash between Yü-wen Hu's filial obligations to his mother and his political obligations to the state is in one sense a Confucian cliché, it is also a provocative empirical instance of one result when traditional moral modes were not easily harmonized with the contrary demands of political reality.

The biography of Yü-wen Hu, then--doubtless colorful and dramatic enough in its portrayal of Hu's political fortunes and of the ironic circumstances of his death--goes beyond the merely "picturesque." It also illustrates human resourcefulness within the bounds of historical precedent and illuminates patterns and dynamics in Chinese history.

Notes to Introduction

1. The text of the translation offered below is the biography of Yü-wen Hu in Chou shu 周書 11.1a-17b. His biography also appears in Pei shih 北史 57.3a-11a.

2. There are various explanations as to which Altaic word the name Yü-wen transcribes. It may go back to a form related to Mongol ebüsün 'grass' or emüne 'south.' For a discussion of this problem, see Chou Yi-liang, "On the Racial Origin of the Yüwen of Chou," Chung-yang yen-chiu yüan li-shih yü-yen yen-chiu so chi-k'an 中央研究院歷史語言研究所集刊 VII (1939), 512-513; Peter A. Boodberg, "Marginalia to the Histories of the Northern Dynasties, I-II," HJAS, III (1938), 244, n. 67; also L. Bazin, "Recherches sur les parlers T'o-pa," TP, XXXIX (1950), 297.

3. WS 103.22a-b describes the habits of the Yü-wen in some detail and gives Liao-tung 遼東 as their homeland. CS 1.1a says they came from Liao-hsi 遼西. Chou Yi-liang (op. cit.) has assembled the pertinent material and made a strong case for identifying the Yü-wen clan as Hsiung-nu, rather than Hsien-pei. While PS 98.2a says their language was somewhat different from that of the Hsien-pei, Sui shu 61.1a identifies them as Hsien-pei. Other contradictions also remain. Chou Yi-liang (pp. 516-517) makes the point that if the Yü-wen originally were Hsiung-nu, they may have attempted to conceal this because of the low esteem in which the Hsiung-nu were held after the rise of the T'o-pa Wei.

4. Shiratori Kurakichi 白鳥庫吉, in his article "Tōgo min-zoku kō" 東胡民族考, Shigakuzasshi 史學雜誌, XXII.1

-Notes to pp. 2-3-

(1911), 81-84, while relying chiefly on Je-ho chih 熱河志 57.6b and Tu-shih fang-yü chi-yao 讀史方輿紀要 18.46b, has gleaned some interesting material about the Yü-wen from various sources. He established that the Yü-wen tribes, circa 280-289, had migrated into an area of southwestern Manchuria. That is stated in a general way in CS, and implied in WS.

5. CS has 侯 (= 俟?) 豆歸, while WS 103.23b has 逸豆歸. Feng Chia-sheng 馮家昇, in his article "Ch'i-tan ming-hao k'ao-shih" 契丹名號考釋, Yen-ching hsüeh-pao, No. 13 (1933), pp. 1-48, has attempted to see in this name, and in others of the early Yü-wen, the source of the designation Ch'i-tan. This hypothesis is repeated in Karl A. Wittfogel and Feng Chia-sheng, History of Chinese Society: Liao (Philadelphia, 1949), p. 1, n. 10. The material in the histories warrants the statement that the Ch'i-tan emerge as a group after the Yü-wen confederation was destroyed by Mu-jung Huang, but we cannot speak of a genetic relationship between the Yü-wen and the Ch'i-tan. Further, the names or titles treated by Feng, i-tou-kuei, ch'i-te-kuei, hsi-tu-kuan, etc., show a close similarity, but the differing initials *i-, *k-, and *s- cannot be glossed over lightly. For example, there is no point in referring to 于 in the transcription of Khotan as a case of a "y" transcribing a "k", since the transcription dates back to the Han, when the initial may have had guttural qualities (cf. Karlgren's archaic *gi̯wo). The use of 俟 in transcriptions is discussed by Pelliot, "Neuf notes sur des questions d'Asie centrale," TP, XXVI (1929), 225-229. The WS version would seem to point to a vocalic initial for the CS character.

6. PS 98.20a. Mu-jung Huang is known as Mu-jung Yüan-chen

元真 in WS 95.26b, to avoid the tatooed name of T'o-pa Huang, an emperor of the Wei (Chou Yi-liang, pp. 505-506). The date follows TCTC 97.7b, but PS 98.20a (WS 103.24a) has 345. Otto Franke, Geschichte des chinesischen Reiches, II, 71, and Gerhard Schreiber, "The History of the Former Yen Dynasty," Monumenta Serica, XIV (1949-55), 470-471, also gives 344. Ch'ang-li 昌黎 was in the area of Lung-ch'eng 龍城, the new capital of the Yen (Schreiber, p. 457). These are believed to have been in the area of modern Ch'ao-yang 朝陽 in Jehol (see Franke, III, 262).

7. CS 1.1b. Hsüan-t'u was established in the area of modern Shen-yang 瀋陽, Liaoning Province, during the Han (TSFYCY 37.1a-b and 35b). Wu-ch'uan was a military colony northeast of the Ordos loop. For these garrisons, see E. Balazs, "Le traité économique du 'Souei-chou,'" TP, XLII (1953), 241ff.

8. Franke, II, 215-221, has given a résumé of the events during these troubled years. Wolfram Eberhard, Das Toba-Reich Nordchinas, pp. 252-269, gives a complete account of the uprisings of this period. See also Balazs, pp. 241-262.

9. CS 1.1b. WS 80.15a gives his name as Wei K'o-kuei 衛可瓌. Boodberg (op. cit., pp. 245-246) touches on these events.

10. CS 1.2a.
11. WS 9.27a.
12. WS 9.29b-30a.
13. CS 11.7a-b.
14. WS 9.32a.
15. WS 74.1a-2b.
16. Franke, II, 222-224.
17. WS 10.5b. The Ch'in River flows south and joins the

Yellow River near Lo-yang.

18. CS 1.2b.
19. CS 1.2b-3a, 14.10a-13a.
20. CS 1.3a-4a, 14.13b-14b.
21. CS 14.14b-15a.
22. CS 1.5b-12a, WS 80.21b-23a.
23. CS 1.17a, PCS 1.6b-7b.
24. CS 2.2a-b.
25. CS 2.2b-7b, PCS 2.10b-11a.
26. CS 2.8b-9a, PCS 2.12a-b.
27. CS 48.6b.
28. Franke, II, 170-174.
29. NS 8.11b.
30. CS 2.16b.
31. CS 2.16b-17a, 17.14b-15b; NS 8.8a-9a.
32. CS 2.3a.
33. Balazs (n. 7 above), pp. 271-272.
34. Goodrich, pp. 11-12. The Chou system underwent so many changes, in addition to being atypical, that no systematic attempt was made to describe it. Some material is in CS 16.14b-17a, and CS 24.2b-5b contains a brief list of titles. Sui shu 27.20b-21b has a few words on the subject.
35. Hu at this time (556) was in his early forties, but the exact year of his birth is not certain, although there are four references to it in his biography. CS 11.17a tells us he was born in the year of the snake, which would correspond to 513. In this same passage, his older brother Tao is said to have been born in 511, and CS 10.2b reports Tao died in 554 at the (Chinese) age of 44, which would confirm it. However, according to other passages in his

biography, Hu was eleven in 524, twelve in 526, and seventeen in 531. Assuming that these references conform to the Chinese style of reckoning age, they would give as the year of Hu's birth 514, 515, and 515 respectively. This matter is discussed in Boodberg (op. cit.), pp. 246-247.

36. CS 15.16a-b; TCTC(166.29a-31a, 167.1a-9a) deals with the events of this period.

37. The news of Yü-wen T'ai's death brought rebellion to many parts of the state; see, for example, CS 35.11b.

38. Between 565 and 568 Yü-wen Kuei 貴 is said to have recommended to Hu that he step down from office, but Hu "was unable to accept this advice" (CS 10.4b). For another instance, see TCTC 171.3a. It is interesting to note that even after Hu's fall, the earlier plots against him were still considered as threats to the state, rather than attacks against his person. An indication of this is that two of his informers, Yü-wen Sheng and Chang Kuang-lo, continued to hold high posts after 572. On the other hand, Hsüeh Shan 薛善, who had informed on someone criticizing Hu, was given the posthumous name of Miu kung 繆公 ("Deluded Duke") by Emperor Wu (CS 35.22a).

39. One of the political features of this period was the influence of the northern tribes on the internal affairs of China. The Western Wei supported the rise to power of the T'u-chüeh because the Juan-juan, who were enemies of the T'u-chüeh, seemed friendly with the eastern state. In 551 a Chinese bride was sent by the Western Wei to T'u-men 土門, the qan of the T'u-chüeh, and in 552 the T'u-chüeh inflicted a severe defeat on the Juan-juan, their former masters. T'u-men was followed successively by his three sons, one of whom, Mu-han 木杆 Qaghan (553-572),

was a great leader and made the T'u-chüeh empire an important one. In 556 plans to have a daughter of his marry Yü-wen T'ai were upset by the death of T'ai. In 563 arrangements were made to send another daughter to become the wife of Yü-wen Yung. Efforts of the Ch'i state to have the girl sent to them were frustrated by the Chou, and at the same time the aid of the T'u-chüeh against the Ch'i was requested. (See E. Chavannes, Documents sur les T'ou-kiue occidentaux, pp. 220 and 260; CS 50.3a-6b.)

40. For a different view of Yü-wen T'ai's intentions in restoring the ancient Chou, see Ch'en Yin-k'o, Sui-T'ang chih-tu yüan-yüan lüeh-lun kao 隋唐制度淵源略論稿 (Academia Sinica, Institute of History and Philology, Monograph Series, 1946), pp. 43-44, 90-91.

41. Shu ching 13.11b.

42. CS 11.3a-b; see p. 30 below.

43. CS 11.4a; see p. 32 below.

44. CS 11.5b; see p. 36 below.

45. CS 16.12a-b.

46. CS 12.4a.

47. CS 10.5a.

48. The "Essay on the Rise and Fall of the Later Chou" Hou Chou hsing-wang lun 後周興亡論 by the sixth century historian, Lu Ssu-tao 盧思道 (535-586), in Ch'üan Sui wen 全隋文 16.12a, states that the downfall of Yü-wen Hu stemmed from his usurpation of imperial authority. Kuang Hung-ming chi 廣弘明集 (664 A.D.), Taisho Daizōkyō 52.125c, says that eighteen of Hu's sons and six high officials were executed together with Hu.

49. See n. 40.

Translation (Chou shu 11.1a–17b, 22b–23b)

fol. 1a [Yü-wen] Hu [宇文]護, the Duke of Chin 晉公, [posthumous name] Tang 蕩, cognomen Sa-pao 薩保,[1] was the youngest son of Hao 顥, the Duke of Shao 邵,[2] [posthumous name] Hui 惠. [The latter was] the elder brother of T'ai-tsu 太祖.[3] As a youth, [Hu] was foursquare and upright[4] and had purpose and capacity. He was especially loved by Emperor Te-huang 德皇[5] and in this respect differed from his elder brothers.

When he was eleven years of age (sui 歲) (524), Duke Hui passed away.[6] [Hu then] followed his uncles into the army of Ko Jung 葛榮. After Jung was defeated, [Hu] was removed to Chin-yang 晉陽.[7] When T'ai-tsu entered [the region inside] the passes, Hu, because of his youth, did not follow him.

At the beginning of the P'u-t'ai 普泰 period (531) he arrived at P'ing-liang 平涼[8] from Chin-yang. He was then seventeen (sui). As all the sons of T'ai-tsu were without exception young, T'ai-tsu entrusted Hu with the family affairs. Inside [the household] and out, without his being severe, all became orderly. Once T'ai-tsu sighed and said, "This boy resembles me in his purpose and capacity."

fol. 1b When [T'ai-tsu] was sent out to oversee Hsia Prefecture 夏州,[9] he left Hu behind to serve Ho-pa Yüeh 賀拔岳.[10] After Yüeh was murdered [in 534], T'ai-tsu came to P'ing-liang and made Hu a Governor-director (tu-tu 都督).[11] [Hu] joined in the punitive expedition against Hou-mo-ch'en Yüeh 侯莫陳悅 and subdued him.[12] Afterwards, because of his meritorious achievement in escorting the Wei emperor, he was enfeoffed as Baron of Shui-ch'ih District 水池縣,[13] with an appanage of five hundred households.

At the beginning of the Ta-t'ung 大統 period (535-551) he was awarded the additional title of Cavalier Attendant with Direct Access (t'ung-chih san-chi ch'ang-shih 通直散騎常侍)[14] and General who Campaigns against the Caitiff (cheng-lu chiang-chün 征虜將軍).[15] Because of his merit gained by participating in the fixing of the [ritual] music, he was advanced in feudal status, being made a duke, and his appanage was increased from the previous number to one thousand households. He followed T'ai-tsu in capturing Tou T'ai 竇泰,[16] reoccupying Hung-nung 弘農, destroying [the enemy at] Sha-yüan 沙苑, and fighting at Ho-ch'iao 河橋,[17] and in all these he had achievement. He was promoted to [the posts of] General who Garrisons the East (chen-tung chiang-chün 鎮東將軍) and Great Governor-director (ta tu-tu 大都督).[18] In the eighth year (542) he was advanced to Great General of Chariots and Cavalry with Dignities Equal to those of the Three Ministers (ch'e-chi ta-chiang-chün i-t'ung san-ssu 車騎大將軍儀同三司).[19]

In the border campaign of the Mang Hills 邙山,[20] Hu was surrounded by men of the enemy forces while leading a host as vanguard. Because Governor-director Hou-fu-hou Lung-en 侯伏侯龍恩[21] put himself forward to block and ward off [the enemy], [Hu] at this moment gained his escape. As the armies of Chao Kuei 趙貴[22] and others had also retreated by this time, T'ai-tsu withdrew his troops. Hu was implicated and removed from office, but soon after he was restored to his original position.

In the twelfth year (546) he was awarded the additional title   fol. 2a
of Great General of Cavalry (p'iao-chi ta-chiang chün 驃騎大

將軍)²³ [conjoined] with Palatine with Dignities Equal to those of the Three Ministers (k'ai-fu i-t'ung san-ssu 開府儀同三司).²⁴ He was also advanced and enfeoffed as Duke of Chung-shan²⁵ and his appanage was increased by four hundred households.

In the fifteenth year (549) he was sent out to garrison Ho-tung 河東²⁶ and promoted to [the rank of] Great General. [In 554] with Yü Chin 于謹 he conducted a punitive expedition against Chiang-ling 江陵.²⁷ Hu led light cavalry to form the vanguard. After riding day and night, he sent assistant commanders to storm the cities and garrisons of the Liang [dynasty] overlooking the border. All of these they took. They also captured [Liang's] scouting cavalry, and, advancing their troops directly ahead, arrived under the walls of Chiang-ling.

[The people] inside the city had not expected the arrival of troops. They became fearful and panicky and "were not able to take proper measures."²⁸ Hu then dispatched two thousand cavalry to cut off the river fords and collect the boats and warships in order to prepare for the arrival of the bulk of the troops. After they had surrounded and taken [Chiang-ling], because of [Hu's] achievement his son Hui 會 was enfeoffed as Duke of Chiang-ling.²⁹

Previously the leaders of the Man [tribes] of Hsiang-yang 襄陽蠻, Hsiang T'ien-pao 向天保 and others with over ten thousand families, had taken advantage of the narrow gorges to prepare obstructions.³⁰ When the troops were returning, Hu led his army to chastise them and put them down.

When the six offices [of the Chou] were first put into effect, [Hu] was appointed Assistant Minister of Public Works (hsiao ssu-k'ung 小司空).³¹

While on a western inspection trip, T'ai-tsu reached Ch'ien-t'un Mountain 牽屯山 and became ill.³² He summoned Hu by post courier. Hu saw T'ai-tsu when he reached Ching Prefecture 涇州,³³ but T'ai-tsu was already weak and far gone in his illness. He said to Hu, "Now that I look like this, it is certain that I will not get over it. All my sons are young and small. The outlaws and bandits are not yet quiescent. I entrust to you [the direction of] the affairs of the realm. You ought to exert your strength to accomplish my purpose." Hu, overflowing with tears, accepted the charge. They had reached Yün-yang 雲陽 in their journey when T'ai-tsu expired.³⁴ Hu kept this a secret. Only after he had reached Ch'ang-an 長安 did he proclaim mourning.

At this time, the heir-apparent was of young and tender age.³⁵ There were strong enemies in the neighborhood, and the feelings of the people were not at ease. Hu [grasped] the reins of government inside [the capital] and out [in the provinces] and calmed and made complaisant the civil and military [officials]. Thereupon the minds of the people were put at rest.

Before this, T'ai-tsu had often said, "I will have [for support] the strength of the Hu 胡 (barbarians)." At that time no one understood his meaning. At this point men took the [almost homophonous] word hu 護 [of Hu's name] for it.³⁶ Shortly after he was installed as Pillar of State (chu-kuo 柱國).³⁷

When T'ai-tsu's grave mound was completed, Hu considered that the Heavenly mandate [of the Wei] had completed its cycle. He sent men to suggest this to the Wei emperor, and the formalities of abdication and succession were subsequently carried out.³⁸ When Emperor Hsiao-min 孝閔 ascended the throne, he installed [Hu] as Great Constable (ta ssu-ma 大司馬)³⁹ and

fol. 2b

fol. 3a enfeoffed him as Duke of the State of Chin, with an appanage of ten thousand households.[40]

Chao Kuei, Tu-ku Hsin 獨孤信,[41] and others plotted a surprise attack on Hu. Hu took advantage of Kuei's entering the court to seize him and his party, and all of them were subdued and executed.[42] [Hu] was then installed as Great Chancellor (ta chung-tsai 大冢宰).[43]

By this time, the General Accountant (ssu-hui 司會) Li Chih 李植,[44] the Army Constable (chün ssu-ma 軍司馬) Sun Heng 孫恆,[45] and others who in T'ai-tsu's court had long occupied [positions of] authority and importance, upon seeing Hu seize control, feared they would not be retained. They secretly called together the Major-domo (kung-po 宮伯) I-fu Feng 乙弗鳳,[46] Chang Kuang-lo 張光洛, Ho-pa T'i 賀拔提, Yüan Chin 元進,[47] and others as confidants and had them say to the Emperor: "Since the time when Hu executed Chao Kuei, his influence and authority have daily increased. Clever ministers and veteran officers vie in going and attaching themselves to him. All administrative matters, large and small, are decided by Hu. As we your servants see it, he will not maintain the dutifulness of a [loyal] minister. We fear his unrestrained growth and desire to deal with him in time."[48] The Emperor agreed with their words.

fol. 3b Feng and the others further said, "The former king, even with his sagacity and intelligence, still [saw the need to] entrust to Chih 植 and Heng 恆 the administrative affairs of the court. If now these two [continue] on your left and right to assist in carrying [the burden of the state] there will be success in every direction. But the Duke of Chin frequently says, 'I now flank and support the throne. I desire to conduct affairs as did the Duke of Chou.' We your servants have heard that the Duke of Chou controlled the regency government for seven years. Only after this did he 'restore [the management of affairs] to the child, the intelligent prince.'[49] How could Your Majesty endure [this state of affairs] as it is today for seven years? We deeply desire that you not doubt us." The Emperor believed them even more.

Several officers and warriors exercised and practised in the rear gardens to perfect their ability to seize someone and bind him. Hu secretly learned of this,[50] and, desiring to put an end to their plot, sent out Chih to become Prefect (tz'u-shih 刺史) of Liang Prefecture 梁州 and Heng to become Prefect of T'ung Prefecture 潼州.[51]

Later, the Emperor thought of Chih and the others and desired to summon each of them. Hu remonstrated with him, saying, "In the whole world, there is no closer relationship than that of elder and younger brother. If even brothers come to the point of suspicion and rupture, how can one easily be close to other men? Because Your Majesty was young in years,[52] T'ai-tsu in his testamentary charge entrusted to me, your servant, the [direction of] affairs after [his death]. Since your servant's feelings are bound up with both the family and the state, he has truly desired to exert to the utmost [the strength] of his limbs. If Your Majesty were yourself to take charge of the myriad affairs of state, causing your majestic influence to spread over all within the Four Seas, [your servant would rejoice in] his own day of death as if it were his year of birth. But your servant fears that after his removal, treachery and depravity will be able to act in their own interest. Not only will it not profit Your Majesty, but also [your servant] fears the altars of the soil and grain[53] will be endangered [and even] ruined. The reason your servant has hustled and bustled and thus has interfered

fol. 4a

with your heaven-endowed majestic influence is only so that he might not fail T'ai-tsu's testamentary trust to protect and keep safe the good fortune of the state. I had not supposed that Your Majesty would not understand your ignorant servant's sincerity and honesty, and that thus there would arise doubts and a barrier [between us]. Moreover, since your servant was already the elder brother of the Son of Heaven, in addition to being the chancellor of the state, for what else could he care to seek and to entertain expectations? I humbly desire that Your Majesty will have the means to understand your servant and not be misled by the speech of slanderous men." Thereupon [Hu] cried and wept for a long time before ceasing. The Emperor still doubted him.

Feng and the others were even more alarmed, and their secret plots increased in number and scope. Subsequently they set a day on which to summon the group of nobles to come in [to the court] for a feast; they were then going to seize Hu and execute him. [Chang] Kuang-lo reported their past and future plans to Hu in full detail. Hu then summoned the Pillar of State, Ho-lan Hsiang 賀蘭祥,[54] the Assistant Constable (<u>hsiao ssu-ma</u> 小司馬) Yü-ch'ih Kang 尉遲綱,[55] and others, and reported Feng's plot to them. Hsiang and the others exhorted Hu to depose the Emperor.

Kang was then in general command of the palace troops.[56]
fol. 4b Hu accordingly sent Kang to enter the palace and summon Feng and the others for a discussion of [state] affairs. As they emerged they were seized one by one and brought to Hu's residence. He thereupon dismissed and disbanded the imperial bodyguard, and sent Hsiang to compel the Emperor to be confined to his former town-house.

-Translation- -37-

After all this he bade the various dukes and notables all to assemble. With flowing tears Hu said, "When the late king rose [to high position] from [the status of a commoner in] coarse linen garments, he personally went into battle and 'toiled and labored'[57] for the royal endowment for thirty-odd years. The robbers and bandits were not yet pacified when he suddenly forsook the myriad kingdoms [of this world]. As the position of my humble self at that time was that of a nephew, I personally received his testamentary charge. Because the Duke of Lüeh-yang 畧陽[58] then occupied the position of rightful heir,[59] with you, sirs, I established him [as emperor] and served him. We removed the Wei and raised the Chou to be master within the Four Seas. But from the time of his accession, his excesses and dissoluteness have been without measure. He has become intimately attached to a 'herd of mean creatures,'[60] and put his near and dear at a distance and shunned them. He desires to execute and exterminate all the great ministers and important generals. If these plots were accordingly carried out, the altars of the soil and grain would surely collapse and be overthrown. How then could I face the former king after my death?[61] Today, I would turn my back on [the Duke of] Lüeh-yang [rather than] turn my back on the altars of the soil and grain. The Duke of Ning-tu 寧都[62] is vigorous both in years and virtue. He is benevo- fol. 5a
lent, filial, sagelike and merciful. Within the Four Seas, all turn their hearts [toward him].[63] In the myriad regions, all fix their thoughts [on him].[64] Now I desire to depose the benighted and establish the enlightened. You sirs, what do you think?" The group of ministers all said, "This is an affair of your family. We dare not but hearken to your commands."[65]

Thereupon Feng and others were beheaded outside the gate, and at the same time Chih, Heng, and others were executed. A short while later, he also had the Emperor assassinated.[66] He then escorted Shih-tsung 世宗 from Ch'i Prefecture 岐州 and established him [on the throne].[67]

In the second year (558) [Hu] was installed as Grand Tutor (t'ai-shih 太師)[68] and was given an imperial chariot and ceremonial cap and gown.[69] His son Chih 至 was enfeoffed as Duke of Ch'ung-yeh Commandery 崇業郡.[70] Previously the [title of the office of] Prefect of Yung Prefecture 雍州 had been changed to Warden (mu 牧).[71] Hu was now appointed to administer it,[72] and he was also presented with the musical [instruments] of metal and stone.[73]

In the first year of the Wu-ch'eng 武成 period (559)[74] Hu memorialized that the administration be returned [to the Emperor]. The Emperor granted this,[75] but the important affairs of army and state were still entrusted to Hu.[76]

The Emperor by nature was clever, shrewd, and perceptive. Hu was deeply afraid of him. There was a certain Li An 李安[77] who had originally obtained favor from Hu by virtue of [his culinary skill with] tripod and trencher. He was gradually advanced and elevated in position, reaching Lower Grandee of the Imperial Kitchen (shan-pu hsiao-ta-fu 膳部小大夫).[78] At this time, therefore, Hu secretly ordered An to make use of his offering food to the Emperor and add poisonous drugs to it. The Emperor subsequently took to his sickbed and passed away.[79] Hu [then] established Kao-tsu 高祖[80] [on the throne]. "The officers all attended to their several duties, taking instructions from" Hu.[81]

Ever since Tʻai-tsu had been made Chief Minister (chʻeng-hsiang 丞相) twelve armies had been set up on the left and right, all of which were attached to the Minister's court. After Tʻai-tsu had passed away, they had in every case accepted Hu's decisions and arrangements. Of all that was received [by levy] or sent out, nothing was done without Hu's signature. At Hu's residence the encamped troops and bodyguard were more numerous than at the [imperial] palace gates. Affairs, without [distinction as to] great or small, were first decided on [by Hu] and then heard [by the Emperor].

In the first year of the Pao-ting 保定 period (561)[82] Hu was made Governor-director of Internal and External Military Affairs, and the five bureaus were ordered placed under the Office of Heaven.[83] Someone anticipating Hu's intentions said, "As the virtue of the Duke of Chou was great, [the state of] Lu set up King Wen's ancestral temple. We consider Hu's achievements to be comparable to those of the Duke of Chou, and it is proper to use this ritual." It was thereupon proclaimed that at Tʻung Prefecture 同州,[84] at [Hu's] residence in Chin state, there should be set up a separate ancestral temple for Emperor Te-huang, and Hu was to sacrifice in it.

In the third year (563) an imperial proclamation said, "The great Chancellor, the Duke of Chin, with his wisdom embraces the myriad things, and with his Way saves the world.[85] It is by these means that he has been able to bring to completion our imperial patrimony and to provide peace and nourishment for our people. Furthermore, since in his relationship [to me] he is my admirable elder brother and in his responsibilities he serves as my principal support, how can he be of the same class

fol. 6a

as the throng of courtiers and equal in rank with the host of vassals? From now on the proclamations and pronouncements, and likewise the documents of the various bureaus, must not mention the Duke's personal name, in order to manifest a special courtesy." Hu objected to the memorial and strenuously declined [this honor].[86]

Previously when T'ai-tsu was laying the foundation of the patrimony, he made a marriage alliance with the T'u-chüeh, planning thus to effect a front-and-rear [strategy][87] so as to deal jointly with the Kao family.[88] Accordingly, in this year (563) the Pillar of State, Yang Chung 楊忠,[89] was sent with the T'u-chüeh eastward to attack. They broke through the long wall of the Ch'i,[90] reached Ping Prefecture 并州, and returned, with the expectation that they would mobilize again the next year, with co-ordinated movements from the south and north. The Ch'i ruler was greatly alarmed.[91]

Before this, Hu's mother Madam Yen 閻姬, together with the imperial fourth aunt and various other members of the family, had all alike fallen into the hands of Ch'i, and all of them had been imprisoned.[92] After Hu became chief minister, each time he sent secret couriers to investigate and search no one had any news of them. It now came to pass that all were allowed to return to the court, and [Ch'i] also made a request for a reconciliation.[93]

fol. 6b In the fourth year (564) the imperial aunt was the first to arrive. The Ch'i ruler, because Hu then filled a position of authority and importance, retained his mother to serve as a later check. Subsequently they ordered someone, on behalf of [Madam] Yen, to compose a letter addressing Hu as follows:[94]

"Heaven and earth are separated and obstructed; son and mother are in different places. For thirty odd years[95] we have been cut off from one another like the living from the dead. The anguish of my bowels cannot be overcome. I think then of the sadness in your heart [and wonder] how you can bear it.

"I can recall when at nineteen I entered your household. Now I am already eighty. I have met with loss and calamities, and have experienced all kinds of difficulties and perils, but I have always hoped that when all of you were grown up, I would see a day of tranquillity and joy. How could I have foreseen that my crimes and offences would be [considered] so deep and heavy that I would be separated from both the living and the dead? In all I gave birth to three boys and three girls.[96] Today I do not see a single one of you before my eyes. When I come to speak of this, sorrow entwines my flesh and bones.

"Owing to the benevolence and pity of the imperial Ch'i, my declining years are made somewhat peaceful. Moreover, I have had your paternal aunt Madame Yang 楊,[97] your paternal aunt née Ho-kan 紇干, your elder brother's wife the bride née Liu 劉, and others to live together with me.[98] It has been rather agreeable to me, but because I have a slight infirmity of the ears, fol. 7a I can only hear when people speak loudly. In movement and eating, fortunately, I have no great indisposition.

"Today the sagacity and virtue of the great Ch'i have extended afar, and they have specially conferred on me their profound mercy. They not only promise my return to you, but also allow me first to send tidings to you. I had accumulated [through the years] an enduring grief, but now it has been dispelled without a trace. This is indeed benevolence equal to that of the Creator.

How shall we ever repay their virtue?

"At the time when you and I parted, you were still young. The family affairs prior to that are perhaps not known to you in detail. Formerly, in Wu-ch'uan Garrison 武川鎮, I gave birth to you and your brothers. The eldest was born in the year of the Rat, the next, in that of the Hare, and you yourself in that of the Snake.

"On the day that Hsien-yü Hsiu-li 鮮于修禮 arose, our whole family, large and small, had been living in Po-ling Commandery 博陵郡. Traveling together, we desired to go to Tso-jen City 左人城. When we had traveled to the north of the T'ang River 唐河, we were attacked and defeated by the official army of Ting Prefecture 定州.[99] Your grandfather and second uncle were both lost in battle at that time. Your paternal aunt née Ho-pa 賀拔 and her son Yüan-pao 元寶, your aunt née Ho-kan and her son P'u-t'i 菩提,[100] as well as you and I, six in all, were captured and taken into the city of Ting Prefecture. After a short time they took you and me and handed us over to Yüan Pao-chang 元寶掌.[101] [The ladies née] Ho-pa and Ho-kan were each separated and sent away [to different places.]

"When Pao-chang saw you, he said, 'I knew his venerable grandfather. In aspect and bearing they are very much alike.' At that time Pao-chang was encamped inside T'ang City 唐城, and he tarried there for three days. Pao-chang took captive about sixty or seventy men and women,[102] all of whom were escorted toward the capital. At this time I was escorted with you. When we stopped, we had arrived south of the chief city of Ting Prefecture. We lodged for the night at the house of Chi K'u-ken 姫庫根,[103] who was of the same village as we. A

fol. 7b

Ju-ju 楂茹 slave[104] espied in the distance the campfires of Hsien-yü Hsiu-li and said to me, 'I will now go to our own army.' When he got to the camp, he told them where all of us were. At sunrise the next day your uncles led troops to meet and intercept you, me and the others, and took us back to their camp. At this time you were twelve years of age. Together we mounted horses to follow the army. Perhaps you do not remember the details of this affair.

"Afterwards, you and I dwelt together in Shou-yang 受陽.[105] fol. 8a
During this time, Yüan-pao, P'u-t'i and your paternal aunt's son, Ho-lan Sheng-lo 賀蘭盛洛,[106] as well as you yourself, making four in all, used to study together. The teacher, whose surname was Ch'eng 成, was severe and hateful as a person. You four boys planned to bring him to harm. I and your paternal aunts heard of this. Each seized her child and spanked him. Only Sheng-lo, who was without a mother, was not spanked.[107]

"Afterwards, in the year [530] when Erh-chu 尒朱 the Pillar of Heaven (t'ien-chu 天柱) fell,[108] Ho-pa A-tou-ni 賀拔阿斗泥[109] was in the area west of [T'ung] Pass.[110] He sent men to escort [back] members of his family. At the same time your uncle also sent a servant Lai Fu 來富 to escort you, Sheng-lo and the others. On this occasion you wore a dark red damask robe and a silver-adorned girdle. Sheng-lo wore a robe made of cloth woven with a purple thread and knotted all over, and having a yellow damask lining. You both mounted mules and left together. Sheng-lo was younger than you. You and the others, three in all,[111] addressed me as a-ma-tun 阿摩敦.[112] You should distinctly remember things like these. Now, moreover, I am sending you the outside layer of a brocaded fol. 8b robe which you wore in your childhood. When it arrives, you ought to examine it, and so realize that I have endured grief and distress extending over a great number of years.

"It was through a kind of luck that occurs once in a thousand years that I met with the kindness of the great Ch'i. Having compassion for the aged and showing benevolence, they have allowed us to see each other. At once, upon hearing these words, even the dead would cease to decay;[113] how much stronger is the case with us, now that we shall surely be brought together!

"Among the birds, beasts, plants and trees mothers and children are near to each other. What crimes had I committed that I was separated from you? Now, on the other hand, through what blessing have I again the hope of seeing you? Speaking of this transition from grief to happiness, it is as if I had died and am now revived.

"All things in the world can be obtained, if they are sought. But if a mother and son are in different states, where can he or she be sought? Even if your honors were beyond those of dukes and princes and your wealth exceeded the mountains and oceans, you still would have an old mother of eighty years, drifting about, a thousand *li* away, about to die at any time without obtaining one morning's short meeting, without obtaining one day of being together with you. When cold I do not get your clothing, and when hungry I do not get your food. Even if your glory reaches the utmost limits, with its brilliance dazzling the world,

fol. 9a how do you use it for me, and what good is it to me? If, where I am concerned, you have been unable, before today, to extend supplies and nourishment, the matter is past and what can be said? From today on, what is left of my life is dependent only on you. Above is heaven, below is the earth,[114] and between there are souls and spirits. Do not say that they are obscure and hidden and that you can deceive and go against them.

"Your paternal aunt Madame Yang can now be sent first despite the intense heat. The passes and rivers, the obstructions and distances have divided us for many years. If this letter were in the ordinary form, I fear that you would doubt [its authenticity]. Therefore in each case I have given the truthful evidence in its entirety and moreover have affixed my name. You ought to understand these circumstances and not consider it strange."

Hu was by nature extremely filial.[115] When he obtained the letter, he could not control his grief. No one about him was able to look upon him. He sent a letter in reply saying:

"The world has collapsed, and we have encountered disasters. I have been away from under your knee[116] for thirty-five years. Those who have received form and have been endowed with life all recognize [the bond between] mother and child. Who is like Sa-pao in being as unfilial as this? Long impending calamities and accumulating disasters should deservedly be visited upon me alone. How could I realize that the web [of retribution] would implicate my loving mother?[117] I could only seek to establish myself in life and order my conduct, not failing in a single thing. The sacred spirits with their intelligence ought to have been pitying and sympathetic. Yet the son became a noble lord and the mother a prisoner. When it is hot I am not aware of my mother's being hot. When it is cold I am not aware of mother's being cold. As for clothing, I do not know whether or not you have any; as for food, I do not know when you are hungry or satiated. You were inaccessible as if beyond heaven and

fol. 9b

earth; there was no way for me to hear you even for an instant. Day and night I cried out with grief, until there were tears of blood.[118] I realized in my heart that this injustice and cruelty would last the whole of this life. If there is any cognition in death, I only hope that I will be able to see you in the nether regions.

"Unexpectedly the Ch'i court opened the net, and graciously accorded us the virtuous words [of the emperor][119] that you, ma-tun,[120] and our fourth paternal aunt are both to be kindly granted release. When I first heard of this intent, my soul and vigor flew out, I called to Heaven and knocked my head on the earth; I could not control myself. The fourth paternal aunt was presently accompanied with decorum [to the border] and peacefully and safely entered our territory.

"In this month, on the eighteenth day, I paid my respects [to her] at Ho-tung.[121] When from a distance I caught a glimpse of her face, it rent and shook my bowels. But having been apart for many years, separated like the living from the dead, when we first saw each other, we could not bear to speak. She only

fol. 10a discussed the great magnanimity of the Ch'i court and how they often possess a great reserve of kindness. She also said that she and you, ma-tun, although living in a guarded palace, were always treated with extraordinary decorum. Now that you have been brought to Yeh 鄴 , the gracious treatment has been even more complete.

"Because of compassion for grief it was granted you, ma-tun, to accord me a letter. It gave in complete detail the sadness and cruelty [of fate] and fully narrated the family affairs. Before I had finished reading it, my five emotions were cut to pieces.

I dare not forget any detail of what you discussed in the letter. You, ma-tun, are of venerable age and in addition have experienced grief and bitterness. I often thought that with inadequate sleep and food [your memory might be such that] you let details slip. When I saw in your letter that every detail was ordered so clearly, on the one hand I was sad, yet on the other I was happy.

"On the day when our native place was destroyed, I, Sa-pao, was over ten years of age (sui). As the past affairs of the old home can still be remembered by me, how much more should [I bear in mind] the calamities of our family and the dispersal and separation of our relatives. When I received your parting words your continual maternal counsels were engraven on my flesh and bones and constantly bound to my heart and bowels.

"Heaven has wrought destruction and disorder, and the four seas have raised rampaging floods. At the time when T'ai-tsu arose, the Ch'i court functioned peacefully. One in the 'Land between the Two Rivers'[122] and the other at the 'Three Props,'[123] each fell in with the divine devices. When we examine the traces of these events, [we find that] there was no mutual failing. When T'ai-tsu ascended to the 'Far Region,' he had not yet made certain the Heavenly Protection.[124] I, Sa-pao, as the eldest of his nephews, personally received his testamentary charge. Although I occupied a position of importance, I held my office as one mournfully bereaved. As we reached the yearly seasonal celebrations, and my sons and grandsons gathered in my courtyard, I looked about mournfully and sadly, [for my mother was not here], and my heart was broken again and again. How could I face the world and bear this shame [of unfilialness] before the divine and sacred [beings]?

fol. 10b

"[Now] the benevolence [of Ch'i] pours down so that we are moistened and saturated by it. The scope of their love and reverence is even extended to outsiders. Even plants and trees have feelings, and beasts and fish are grateful for kindness; how, then, in human relationships can one fail in one's grateful remembrance?

"In maintaining one's family and one's state, sincerity and righteousness are basic. Humbly I should guess that a date must have already been set for you to come over. As soon as I obtain sight of your loving face, my life's desires will be eternally satisfied. [It will be as if] life had been given to the dead and flesh put back on the bones [of the dead].[125] What could surpass this benevolence? Even bearing mountains on one's back and carrying peaks on one's head would not exceed my burden [of gratitude].

fol. 11a "Since the two states are separated, in principle there ought to be no letter-writing [between the two]. The Emperor, as that court had the benevolence not to cut off mother and son, also grants permission to me to offer you an answer. So, unexpectedly, today I am able to send a letter from home. As I proffer this piece of paper with sighs and sobs, [I realize that] my words do not wholly reveal my heart.

"You had delivered to me, Sa-pao, some brocaded silk for a robe which I left behind at the time of parting.[126] Although that was many years ago, I can still recognize it as before. I am embracing it with grief and tears until the time when I see you, rendering the obeisance [due a mother]. It is now as if I were enduring death. What other thought can I have than that of seeing you?"

The Ch'i court did not then send her out, but on the contrary had letters sent to Hu demanding of him a heavy ransom. Messages went to and fro repeatedly and still in the end [Hu's] mother did not arrive. There was a court discussion about their neglect of good faith, and a responsible official was ordered to issue a protest[127] to Ch'i which said:

"He who has righteousness is preserved, but he who lacks good faith cannot stand up [as a ruler].[128] [In comparison to righteousness and good faith] mountains and peaks are insignificant, and weapons and food are not important.[129] Therefore it was by not disregarding a verbal oath that Ch'ung-erh 重耳 enjoyed the throne;[130] it was by not shaming the sacrificial officials [in their pledges to the spirits] that Sui Hui 隨會 made covenants.[131] There has never yet been one who, while shepherding the people and acting as lord over a state, could ignore righteousness and go back on his word many times.[132]

"Since the time when the cosmological numbers were governed by chun 屯 and [ming] i [明]夷[133] and the period coincided with destruction and separation, there have been three cycles, during which relatives of the imperial family have been engulfed and lost.[134] The honorable paternal aunt and the aunt by marriage[135] had given up hope of returning alive. Your court at the beginning of last summer disclosed virtuous words [of the Emperor] on this matter. You have already escorted back the honorable paternal aunt and promised the return of the aunt by marriage. But then, on claim of wearisome summer heat, you indicated the possibility of her return in the coming fall.

fol. 11b

"We supposed that your good faith was from the heart[136] and that your excellent words would be [realized] without fail. Now the falling leaves warn of the [severe] season, and the ice and frost will soon come. You still deceitfully fabricate false tales about our aunt, and, while not yet discussing any proposals for her return, only seek more reward from us. 'Women, gems and silks'[137] are not what should be required in this matter; our keeping the borders peaceful and the people tranquil, however, you say is not to be regarded as a reward. When we carefully examine this proposal [of yours], [we find that] it is entirely contrary to our original agreement. One extends good feeling to others in accordance with the rules of decorum; how can one do so merely for the sake of appeasement? You demand of the son that he be accountable for his honesty, and yet [you] use a relative as a pawn to seek ransom. This truly damages the harmonious atmosphere and has a perverse effect on the heavenly constants.[138]

"[The rule of] our royal house of Chou is [over] the whole realm of T'ai-tsu. How can we disregard the state to care [only] for the family or do harm to its substance for the sake of reputation![139] He who does not cause injury to those whom he nourishes[140] is called a benevolent man. And is it not worth serious consideration to put down the war drum and conceal the spears? If you cause constant wrangling over mere feet and inches and have us both contend over [matters as small as the tip of] an awl or knife,[141] [then it will be as in the ancient examples] when the tiles were shaken [by war drums] at Ch'ang-p'ing 長平 and the state of Chao 趙 was divided in two,[142] or as when armies came out of Han-ku 函谷[143] and Han 韓 was rent into three.[144] How will you remain whole and think it does not affect you?

"The Great Chancellor's position is exalted both as general and minister, and his feelings are tied both to family and state. Yet he gags his grief and swallows blood;[145] even after death he will remain as a wronged spirit. One would think that when [his mother] bites her finger, he should be able to seek her, or that when she leans against the door, he should be able to come in response.[146] We heard only of the excellent beginning; finally there seems to be no worthy conclusion. The numerous lords are stirred up and alarmed, and the imperial armies are angry and disappointed. Not able to be a filial son, he will still be a loyal subject.

"Last year armies from the north entered deep [into your territory] and counted prisoners below your city walls. Although they are said to have withdrawn their troops, their remaining impetus has not yet run its course. Now their steeds are headed southward and they again expect to enter [your territory]. It is our responsibility that we, 'like men of Chin, should take you by the horns.'[147] It has been heard that all the routes are already in a state of military readiness. Not only will there be a northern encounter, but we shall also invade to the south. If by chance you should wish personally to present yourself [in battle], that is our desire. If perhaps you are girding your cities [for defense] and have not yet been able to seek your opponents, at early dawn tomorrow request an interview, and we will maneuver with you sirs.[148]

"A kind act not carried through only adds to deep resentment. That one who loves his own parents should not fail to respect [others][149] is the instruction received from Father Ni 尼父.[150] To have pity and sympathy for the helpless and aged is the principle bequeathed by King Wen of Chou.[151] The [governmental] right of [deciding] exile and return[152] does not apply here. If you were to comply with your innermost searching, how could there be this breach?"

The letter had not yet been sent when the mother arrived.[153] The entire court was merry and joyful, and there was a general amnesty for the empire. Hu and his mother had been widely separated for many years. Now that they had been reunited, all that he supplied and gave her exhausted the utmost of splendor and abundance. At each of the four seasonal and summer and winter solstice celebrations,[154] Kao-tsu led the various relatives to pay their respects as members of the family, and they would drink a toast to her long life. So extremely great was her honor and glory that from of old the like of it had never been heard.

In this year (564) the T'u-chüeh again led a host to the appointed rendezvous.[155] Because the men of Ch'i had just recently handed over the members of the imperial family, Hu did not wish to be immediately engaged in warfare. On the other hand he feared to break his promise to the tribes on the marches as they might again cause border troubles. Not being able to avoid it, he therefore requested an eastern campaign.

In the ninth month a proclamation said:

"Even in the case of one as divine as Hsüan Huang 軒皇 one still tells of three battles,[156] and of a sage like Chi Wu 姬武 one yet speaks of one campaign.[157] The fearfulness of the bow and arrow, the use of the shield and dagger-axes--these being the great implements of emperors and kings,[158] who [therefore] is able to eschew [the use of] arms?[159] When T'ai-tsu augustly received the heavenly enlightenment, he established our royal

fol. 13a

house of Chou. Wherever the sun and moon shine, there were none who did not obey and follow us.[160]

"The Kao clan, committing transgressions at every opportunity, has illicitly taken possession of Ping 并 and Chi 冀.[161] For generations they have been riding the tide of evil, and their rank stench has been distinctly known.[162] August Heaven has been stirred into anger and, using the T'u-chüeh as its instrument, urges them on to plunder [the area of] the Fen 汾 and Chin 晉 [Rivers][163] and sweep up the land without leaving a trace. As in the case of Chi-meng 季孟, the situation [of Ch'i] is hopeless;[164] as in the case of Po-kuei 伯珪, [the territory of the Ch'i] is daily dwindling.[165] They can only sit and await their extinction. This is known to both the foolish and the wise.

"Therefore, though the T'u-chüeh have withdrawn their troops, they still are camped on the enemy borders [of the Ch'i].[166] Again they gather their various tribes, which all come at once, pouring forth from their country. With the speed of falling stars and the shock of lightning, they will advance together by several roads. The appointed time shall be in the second month of winter, and we shall meet at Ping and Yeh 鄴.[167]

"The Great Chancellor and Duke of Chin is Our admirable elder brother. His responsibilities are more exalted than those of I 伊 and Lü 呂.[168] The pacification and unification of the universe are only to be entrusted to the Duke. We shall personally hold the halberd and battle-ax so that he may respectfully receive them in the ancestral temple. The officials in charge ought to muster the hosts of the troops, estimate their respective distances, and order them to come and assemble in time. All their movements, and their speed of movement, will then be entrusted fol. 13b to the Duke's disposition and decision."

Thereupon they summoned to the court the twenty-four armies,[169] the unattached and the attached troops of the left and right apartments,[170] the soldiers of Ch'in 秦, Lung 隴, Pa 巴, and Shu 蜀,[171] and the hosts of the various border states, amounting to 200,000 men.

In the tenth month[172] the Emperor gave to Hu the halberd and battle-ax in the ancestral temple. When the army arrived at T'ung Pass, [Hu] sent the Pillar of State, Yü-ch'ih Chiung 尉遲迥,[173] leading 100,000 picked troops to form the advance guard. The Great General Ch'üan Ching-hsüan 權景宣[174] led the troops of the Shan-nan 山南 area[175] to go out to Yü Prefecture 豫州. The Minor Tutor (shao-shih 少師) Yang Piao 楊檦[176] went out to Chih Pass 軹關.[177] Hu slowly advanced, with adjoining encampments, and stationed the army at Hungnung. Chiung attacked and surrounded Lo-yang. The Pillar of State and Duke [of Ch'i, Yü-wen] Hsien [齊]公[宇文]憲,[178] the Duke of the State of Cheng 鄭 Ta-hsi Wu 達奚武,[179] and others[180] encamped at the Mang Hills 邙山. Hu by nature had no talent for military strategy, and moreover this campaign was contrary to his original intention. Therefore, although it was a long time since the troops had been sent out, they had subdued and captured nothing. Hu had originally ordered a channel dug to cut off the road on the north side of the river so as to stop the enemy's relief troops. Thus when a concerted attack was later made on Lo-yang, it would have the effect of breaking off communications in and out [of the city]. The various generals as-

fol. 14a sumed that the Ch'i troops would certainly not dare to come forth, except for reconnaissance patrols. But it happened that for successive days it was cloudy and foggy, and the Ch'i cavalry appeared directly in front of the army besieging Lo-yang. At once [the Chou troops] melted and scattered. Only Yü-ch'ih Chiung led several tens of cavalry to oppose the enemy. [Yüwen] Hsien, the Duke of Ch'i, also directed the various generals in the Mang Hills to oppose them and so was able to return with his whole army.[181]

Ch'üan Ching-hsüan had attacked and taken Yü Prefecture. Then because the siege of Lo-yang was lifted, he also led his troops in retreat. Yang Piao was lost in battle at Chih Pass. Hu thereupon withdrew his troops. Because they had failed to achieve anything, he and the other generals kowtowed and requested punishment. However the Emperor did not reprimand them.

In the second year of the T'ien-ho 天和 period (567) Hu's mother died. Soon after there was a decree that he be summoned and ordered to attend to his office.

In the fourth year (569) Hu made a tour of inspection of the cities and military posts of the northern border, went as far as Ling Prefecture 靈州,[182] and then returned.

In the fifth year (570) there was again an imperial proclamation, which said:

"When glory abode at Ch'ü-fu 曲阜,[183] Lu employed the music of the suburban sacrifices to heaven.[184] When [the emanations of] the earth took a position corresponding to Shen-hsü 参墟,[185] Chin had the ritual of the great hunt.[186] By these means were services bespoken, estimated according to the season,[187] and thus also was virtue displayed and conduct recorded. The Imperial Commissioner Holding the Seal of Command,

Grand Tutor (t'ai-shih 太師), Governor-general of Internal and External Military Affairs, Pillar of State, Great General, Great Chancellor and Duke of the State of Chin, embodies the Way and dwells in uprightness.[188] He incorporates harmony and spreads abroad his virtue. In position he occupies the most honored place among the relatives,[189] and in talent he has shown the exalted strength of a main beam.[190] As the nation has gone through distress and difficulty,[191] he has shared in all its weals and woes. When the imperial rule was being formed and constructed, with his services he took equal part in both the good and ill fortune. Therefore in his traceless fusion [with the Way] he was near perfection, and in his compliance with Reason he was ' thus benevolent.'[192]

At present the script and wheel-gauges are still not in agreement,[193] the regions and corners [of the empire] are still obstructed, the codes and plans are not yet wholly prepared,[194] and the sonority and splendor [of the Emperor] have many lacunae.[195] Yet it is proper to present to him the music of the [instruments] suspended trilaterally and the dancers in six rows."[196]

Hu was by nature very tolerant and amiable but he was dense as to large situations. He was self-confident on account of his achievement in establishing and setting up [the state] and had long held the position of power and influence. But those whom he had appointed to office were in no case the right men [for the positions]. In addition, his various sons were avaricious and destructive, and his retinue of followers were remiss and irresponsible. Relying on Hu's majestic power, there were none who did not gnaw on the administration and injure the people. Above and below there was mutual deceiving, yet [Hu] never had a suspicious thought [about this state of affairs].

Kao-tsu, because of this rashness and lack of respect, secretly plotted against him with Chih 直, Prince of Wei 衛王.[197] On the eighteenth day of the third month of the seventh year (April 16, 572) Hu returned from T'ung Prefecture. The Emperor went in person to the Hall of Civil Tranquillity (Wen-an tien 文安殿) to receive Hu. When the reception was finished, he led Hu to the Hall of Cherished Benevolence (Han-jen tien 含仁殿) to pay court to the August Empress Dowager.[198]

Previously, whenever the Emperor saw Hu in the imperial quarters, he customarily treated him with the courtesy of a family member. When Hu visited the Empress Dowager, the Empress Dowager was certain to give him a seat, while the Emperor would stand to wait upon him. At this time, when Hu was about to enter, the Emperor spoke to him saying, "Although the Empress Dowager's years are venerable, she has a craving for wine. She does not personally hold court and sometimes she dispenses with interviews. During her periods of joy and anger she is at times perverse. Although recently I have often remonstrated with her to her face, I have not yet experienced the favor of being received. Elder Brother, since you are about to pay court to her, I wish you would once more plead with her and request her [to stop]."

Thereupon he took out from his bosom the "Admonishment on Wine" (Chiu kao 酒誥),[199] and giving it to Hu said, "Use this to remonstrate with the Empress Dowager." When Hu entered, just as the Emperor had enjoined him, he read and explained it to the Empress Dowager. He was not yet finished when the Emperor struck him from behind with a jade scepter. Hu crumpled

fol. 15a

to the ground. [The Emperor] then ordered a eunuch, Ho Ch'üan 何泉,[200] to strike him with the imperial sword. Ch'üan was so frightened and trembling that his strokes were not able to wound [Hu]. At this time Chih, the Prince of Wei, who had previously hidden in a doorway, emerged and beheaded him.

When the Emperor had previously desired to plot against Hu, Wang Kuei 王軌,[201] Yü-wen Shen-chü 宇文神舉,[202] and Yü-wen Hsiao-po 宇文孝伯[203] participated a good deal in the preparation of the plot. On this day, Kuei and the rest were all outside, and no one else knew of it. When the murder of Hu was finished, the Major-domo Chang-sun Lan 長孫覽[204] and others were summoned and informed. Then they were ordered to arrest Hu's sons: Hui, the Pillar of State and Duke of the State of T'an 譚,[205] Chih, the Great General and Duke of the State of Chü 莒,[206] Ching 靜, the Duke of Ch'ung-yeh 崇業,[207] Ch'ien-chia 乾嘉, the Duke of Cheng-p'ing 正平, as well as Ch'ien-chi 乾基, Ch'ien-kuang 乾光, Ch'ien-wei 乾蔚, Ch'ien-tsu 乾祖, Ch'ien-wei 乾威,[208] and the others; also the Pillar of State, Hou-fu-hou Lung-en,[209] Lung-en's younger brother, Great General Wan-shou 萬壽,[210] Great General Liu Yung 劉勇,[211] Cheng Yüan-chieh 正袁傑, Chief Recorder of the Interior and Exterior (chung-wai-fu ssu-lu 中外府司錄) and Duke of Yin 尹,[212] Li An, the Lower Grandee of the Imperial Kitchen[213]--[these] and others in the palace were killed. Hsien, Prince of Ch'i, spoke to the Emperor saying, "Li An came from among the menials.[214] He was only in charge of the kitchen. Since he did not participate in the current administration, there was no sufficient reason to execute him." Kao-tsu said, "You, my lord, do not know. Shih-tsung's demise was An's doing."

On the nineteenth day (April 17) there was an imperial proclamation which said:

"The relatives of a ruler should have no expectations. If they do have expectations, they surely ought to be killed.[215] Hu, the Grand Tutor, Great Chancellor, and Duke of Chin, was by position indeed among our royal kin, and he had moral obligations toward both our family and the state. Since the very founding [of the empire] he shared all our troubles and difficulties. Consequently he was given responsibility for the control of the power of the court and was profoundly trusted with the fate of the state. But he failed to exert his utmost sincerity and to devote all his heart and strength to fulfilling his duty in serving his prince and to displaying sentiments appropriate to the obsequies of the departed [ruler].[216]

"As to Our elder brother, the former Duke of Lüeh-yang,[217] his aura of valor was flourishing and far-reaching and in his mental faculties he was perspicacious. In position he occupied the saintly heirship; in respect to the rites he came 'just over the jade ring.[218] Even while the bequeathed instructions [of Yü-wen T'ai] were still in our ears, a cruel fate was already inflicted on him. For a long time We have thought about this heavy blow, and it has pierced to the very marrow of our bones.

"Shih-tsung, the Emperor Ming-huang 明皇, was full of sagacity and divine gallantry . . .[219] with a store of wisdom. Hu, while inwardly harboring malignancy and contumacy, outwardly took advantage of his elevated position. Who among all the ministers and the people has not felt resentment and indignation? It is thirteen years since We inherited this majestic foundation. We entrusted the government to him as tutor-supporter, and we fol. 16b laid responsibility on his office as chancellor. But Hu's ambition was to deny his ruler, and his principles ran counter to the duties of a subject. Harboring in his bosom this scorpion poison, he gave free rein to that wolf's heart of his. Indulging his passions, he killed and persecuted, and he recklessly displayed his influence and fortune. His clique of friends stirred one another up, and goods used for bribes publicly circulated. Those whom he liked were given down and feathers, while those whom he disliked bore bruises and scars.[220]

"While practicing self-restraint and austere living, in our sentiments We maintained interest in the numerous affairs of government. Yet each time we thought of extending leniency and kindness to those below, he would fail us by obstructing it. This subsequently caused the people to wither and be ruined, and the taxes to become burdensome and oppressive; hence the homes lacked daily provisions, and the people had no means of subsistence.

"Moreover since the three regions had not yet been settled[221] and the borders and corners were still obstructed, the territory within the frontiers had to be kept vigilant under war banners, while the warriors had to supply their strength to defend the city walls. But Hou-fu[-hou] Lung-en, Wan-shou, Liu Yung and others, while they had not yet put into effect any achievements, had already occupied the highest ranks of the officers. [And thus they had] high gates, lofty roofs, and mansions with carved walls.[222] Many indeed were their followers, and, sharing in malevolence, they abetted one another.

"The people had been shown no examples of virtue, hence only profit was their concern. The common people wailed clamorously, and on the roads they [signalled their resentment] with their glances.[223] All sentient beings regarded one another with dread and kept their mouths shut. We constantly feared that the foundation of seven hundred [years][224] would suddenly overturn and sink and that the fate of the masses would all at once[225] be in perilous danger. Above we would then trouble the spirits of our ancestors and below fail in our responsibility to all living beings. Now we have solemnly applied the penal code. Hu is already duly punished. The rest of his evil party have all been subjected to execution. The noxious atmosphere is henceforth cleared, and those near and far share in the rejoicing. The court administration is now renewed and the masses of people can make a new beginning.

"We deem it proper to have a general amnesty for the world, and to change the seventh year of [the reign-title] T'ien-ho to be the first year of Chien-te 建德."[226]

Hu's heir Hsün 訓 had been made Prefect of P'u Prefecture 蒲州.[227] That night [Yü-wen] Sheng [宇文] 盛, Pillar of State and Duke of Yüeh 越,[228] was sent by third-class official carriage[229] to P'u Prefecture to summon Hsün to hasten to the capital. When Hsün reached T'ung Prefecture,[230] he was ordered to commit suicide. Hu's Seneschal (chang-shih 長史) Ch'ih-lo Hsieh 叱羅協 of Tai Commandery 代郡,[231] his Chief Recorder (ssu-lu 司錄) Feng Ch'ien 馮遷 of Hung-nung,[232] and those who were close to him in office, all had their names removed [from the rolls of officialdom]. Hu's son Shen 深, the Duke of Ch'ang-ch'eng 昌城,[233] had been sent to the T'u-chüeh. The Palatine Yü-wen Te 宇文德[234] was now despatched with a sealed decree for his execution on the spot.

In the third year (574) there was an imperial edict restoring to Hu and his sons their previous enfeoffments, and Hu was posthumously called Tang 湯 , "The Unrestrained." They also changed his burial place and reinterred him.

fol. 22b   The historian Your Majesty's subject says:[235]

Chung-ni 仲尼 had a saying, "There are men with whom we can get along in pursuit of the Way but whom we still cannot join in expedient acts."[236] By Way is meant following the correct form. By expedient acts is meant opposing the standards. Following the correct form is a result of normal reason, and
fol. 23a by this means it is easy to accomplish the deeds needed for ministering to the world. Opposition to the standards is related to emergencies, and by this means it is difficult to insure the achievement of setting right one's time. Therefore, if one obtains the [proper] man, there is order. I Yin's 伊尹 banishing of T'ai-chia 大甲 [237] and Tan 旦 of Chou acting as minister to the Tender Youth are examples of this.[238] If one does not obtain such a man, there is disorder. Hsin-tu 新都 removing the tripods of Han[239] and the family of Chin 晉 overthrowing the clan of Wei 魏 are examples of this.[240]

Therefore, the former kings clarified the precedence of high and low, and the sages emphasized the distinction between rulers and subjects. When [vassals] pledged their loyalty, they would serve [their ruler] as his arms and legs.[241] When they received a title they took equal part in good and evil fortune. When they personally received [particular] regard and trust and hence in position occupied the chancellory and directorship,[242] then even the threat of a sharp sword[243] or being placed over a bubbling caldron would not suffice to strike fear into their minds. [The privilege of] possessing the imperial seal or ruling over all within the seas would not suffice to sway their hearts. In the cases of such men as these, certainly their achievements vie with the mountain peaks in their height, and their fame equals the eternity of the vast earth.

When the Chou first received the mandate, Yü-wen Hu truly participated in all the difficulties and hardships. Later, when T'ai-tsu met with his demise, his sons were young and immature. The throng of nobles cherished [only] the desire of equality [among their peers], and the whole world had the intent of turning away their allegiance. The fact that eventually the Chou were able to replace the Wei and secure order out of danger was on account of Hu's strength. fol. 23b

If only he might have added to this correct form and deference, and continued it with loyalty and righteousness! For then there might have come the time for repenting transgressions at the T'ung Palace 桐宮 and the completion of the allotted number of years at the Wei-yang 未央 [Palace];[244] and in that case how could what has been recorded in the former histories be worth mentioning [beside him]? But Hu was deficient in learning and he took as his intimates a throng of inferior men. Influence and fortune he [enjoyed] at his own pleasure, and [imperial] punitive expeditions were sent out on his authority. As a subject he had a mind to deny his ruler, and he did what a ruler of men could not endure. Loyalty and filialness are great duties; yet he had no hesitation in going counter to them. Deposing and murdering one's superiors constitute extreme rebelliousness; yet in doing those things he had no regrets. That he ended with his head and body violently parted and his wives and children slaughtered-- is this not as it should be?

Notes to Translation

1. Sa-pao probably represents a transcription of Skt. sārthavāha "leader of a caravan" or "merchant-chief," which also occurs as an epithet of the bodhisattvas. Sa-pao, in various transcriptions, was the title of the headman of Iranian communities in China before and during the T'ang. For this reason, Hu's cognomen has often been cited as evidence of Zoroastrian influence in the northeast at the time of his birth. See, for example, Ishida Mikinosuke 石田幹之助, "Concerning the Period of the Earliest Propagation of the Zoroastrian Religion and its Initial Extent," Tōhōgaku 東方學, I (1951), 46-53. However, the name of Yü-wen Hu may well represent its Buddhist usage. See Fujita Toyohachi 藤田豐八, "Satsuhō ni tsuite 薩寶について," Shigaku zasshi 史學雜誌, XXXVI (1925), 195-215. There is, finally, the possibility that it represents p'u-sa pao 菩薩保 "Protected by the Boddhisattva."

2. Yü-wen Hao, the eldest brother of Yü-wen T'ai, was killed in 524 and posthumously made Duke of Shao in 561 (CS 5.3b).

3. T'ai-tsu was the temple name of Yü-wen T'ai, the youngest son of Yü-wen Hung 宇文肱. His career is set forth in the first two chapters of the Chou shu and in PS 9.1a-18a.

4. On the moral epithet fang cheng 方正 see R. B. Mather, Biography of Lü Kuang, Chinese Dynastic Histories Translations, No. 7 (Berkeley, 1959), p. 67, n. 12 and authorities there cited.

5. Te-huang was the posthumous name of Yü-wen Hung, the grandfather of Hu. He died in 526 and was given the title in 559 (CS 1.1b-2a).

-Notes to pp. 30-31-

6. The events of these years are discussed in the Introduction, pp. 2-4 above.

7. Chin-yang was northwest of modern T'ai-yüan 太原 in Shansi. The eminent clans, including the Yü-wen family, who might oppose the Erh-chu 爾朱 rule, were all sent to Chin-yang, the center of Erh-chu power (CS 10.9a).

8. P'ing-liang was a short distance southwest of the modern P'ing-liang in central Kansu. It was the headquarters of the army at that time.

9. Hsia Prefecture was two hundred li north of the modern Yü-lin 榆林 in northern Shensi. T'ai occupied Hsia Prefecture in 532 to draw upon the resources of the area in order to strengthen opposition to Kao Huan. This plan had been approved by the Emperor at Lo-yang (CS 1.4a-5a).

10. The role of Ho-pa Yüeh, cognomen A-tou-ni 阿斗泥, in these events is discussed in the Introduction, pp. 5-6 above. His biography is in WS 80.17b-21a, CS 14.9a-15a and PS 49.17a-20b. Yüeh was also from the Wu-ch'uan area, and since the wife of Lien, T'ai's brother, was surnamed Ho-pa, it is possible that T'ai and Yüeh were indirectly related.

11. This title was held by the director of military forces, usually of some specific area. See T'ung-tien 32.185b-c and Hu San-hsing's 胡三省 commentary in Tzu-chih t'ung-chien 167.3a-b. The title was replaced by "general-manager" tsung-kuan 總管 in 559 (TT 32.184c).

12. Hou-mo-ch'en Yüeh's biography is in WS 80.21a-23a and PS 49.20b-21b.

13. Shui-ch'ih District was near the modern Lin-t'ao 臨洮 in western Kansu.

14. The office of Cavalier Attendant (san-chi ch'ang-shih 散騎常侍) was instituted during the Wei-Chin period when two existing titles were combined. It was retained by several succeeding dynasties, with the additional epithet t'ung-chih 通直. The office is said to have been an honorary position, without definite duties, and customarily reserved for "men of declining years;" hence its "gradual supersession." See TT 21.123a-b; also Mather, p. 85, n. 84 with further authorities. The reading chi is given by Kuo-yü tz'u-tien 國語辭典 (reprinted Taiwan, 1953), and Chung-hua ta-tzu-tien 中華大字典 (reprinted Shanghai, 1935), both s. v. san-chi.

15. The General Who Campaigns against the Caitiff was a Wei title. It early fell into disuse in the Western Wei, which accounts for the failure of the works on Chinese institutions to mention it.

16. Tou T'ai's brother and father, like Yü-wen T'ai's brother, had been killed by P'o-liu-han Pa-ling. On Tou T'ai's invasion see Introduction, p. 7 above. Either he was not captured alive or else he killed himself soon after capture. His suicide is mentioned in connection with this defeat. See his biography, PCS 15.1a-2b and PS 54.9a-b; also C. S. Goodrich, Biography of Su Ch'o (Berkeley, 1953), p. 65, n. 44. Distinguish from the Northern Chou general bearing the same name mentioned under the date 576 (CS 6.6a).

17. Hung-nung, near modern Ling-pao 靈寶 in Honan. Sha-yüan, slightly west of modern Ch'ao-i 朝邑 in Shensi, just west of the T'ung Pass. Ho-ch'iao, just north of Meng Ford 孟津 in Honan, a strategic outpost of Lo-yang. They were the sites of three battles fought in 537 and 538. See Introduction, p. 7 above.

18. The first was another Wei title. It is recorded in the Chou shu as being awarded only six times, all in the first decade of the Western Wei. The office of Great Governor-director was similar in function to that of Governor-director; see note 11 above.

19. For this title, see Goodrich, pp. 104-105, n. 242. For some reason, in practice the honorific title for this post almost never included the term k'ai-fu 開府. In only two of the approximately 150 occurrences of the title in the Chou shu (34.3b and 36.3a) is this phrase included.

20. The Mang Hills lie between the Lo and the Yellow Rivers, north of Lo-yang. The campaign has been described in the Introduction, p. 8 above.

21. Hou-fu-hou Lung-en became Pillar of State in 571. He was executed in 572 at the time of Hu's assassination (CS 5.18b and 11.15b). While he has no biography in the standard histories, information about him may be gleaned from the biography of his cousin, Hou Chih 侯植 (CS 29.20b-22a and PS 66.8a-b). He was so closely associated with Hu that their names were linked in a prophecy of their fall from power (CS 47.17b).

22. Chao Kuei has biographies in CS 16.1a-3b and PS 59.1b-2b.

23. Great General of the Cavalry was first used as a title when awarded to Ho Ch'ü-ping 霍去病 in the Han. Until the Sui dynasty, it was one of the highest military titles (TT 34.194c).

24. For Palatine, see Goodrich, pp. 105-106, n. 245.

25. The well-known Chung-shan of this period was at the modern Ting 定 in Hopei, and had been the base for the rebellion of Hsien-yü Hsiu-li. There is a curious statement in CS 33.10a that, during the Wei, Chao Hsiang 趙襄, on becoming Protector

of Chung-shan Commandery 中山郡守, settled his family in Tai 代 (in modern Shansi). Tai contained within it Wu-ch'uan, the home of the Yü-wen family. In this same year, while still Duke of Shui-ch'ih (see n. 13 above), Hu was commissioned to direct the funeral services for his clansman, Yü-wen Ts'e 宇文測 (CS 27.21a).

26. Ho-tung probably refers to the very strategically placed Ho-tung Commandery, in the area of modern Yung-chi 永濟 in Shansi. It later became P'u Prefecture 蒲州, where various of Hu's sons were stationed at one time or another. Hu is mentioned as being stationed in a garrison during this period (CS 25.14b).

27. Yü Chin, cognomen Ssu-ching 思敬, was the commander of this expedition. His biography is in CS 15.9a-19a and PS 23.8b-13b. His full surname was Wan-niu-yü 萬紐于, and he appears under this name in the Liang shu accounts of this campaign. See also CS 32.12a, where he is said to have bestowed this surname on a favorite. The campaign is touched on in the Introduction, p. 9 above. Hu's name appears for the first time in the Chou annals in connection with this expedition (CS 2.16b).

Chiang-ling, at the modern place of the same name in Hupei, was then the capital of Liang.

28. The words shih-t'u 失圖 occur in the Tso chuan, Duke Chao, 7th year (Ch'un-ch'iu 44.5b); see Legge, Chinese Classics, V, 616.

29. Yü-wen Hui was the second son of Hu. In 561 he was made the legal descendant of his grandfather, Hao (CS 5.3b). In 570 Yü-wen Chou 宇文冑, another of Hao's grandsons, and more correctly the heir of Hao, came back from Ch'i. Hui was then

-Notes to p. 32-

made Duke of T'an 譚 公 (CS 5.15a and 10.2a). He was killed with his father in 572.

30. For these Man tribes, see W. Eberhard, Kultur und Siedlung der Randvölker Chinas, T'oung Pao, XXXVI, Supplement (Leiden, 1942), pp. 202-204. Hsiang-yang, which still bears the same name, is on the Han 漢 River in Hupei, almost directly north of Chiang-ling. The Man tribes frequently rebelled against the rule of the Chinese, cutting off the roads passing through the mountain gorges. Hsiang T'ien-pao is not mentioned by name in the section devoted to these people in the Chou shu, but it does state there that one of the three clans of rulers was named Hsiang (CS 49.7a).

According to the section on the Man in the Chou shu, this tribe became stirred up during the Chiang-ling campaign. Tou-lu Ning 豆盧寧, Ts'ai Yu 蔡祐, and other generals were ordered to chastise them, which was done. The next item in the account is dated 555, suggesting at first glance that this campaign took place in 554, the same Chinese year in which Chiang-ling was captured (CS 49.7b). However, since the item dated 555 is concerned with some tribute brought to the capital by a Man tribe, the text does not necessarily imply that the action against the Man occurred in 554. This is borne out by the biography of Ts'ai Yu (CS 27.8b), which places this campaign in 555. No mention of the affair is made in Tou-lu Ning's biography (CS 19.9b), as he was engaged in a more important action against the Liang dynasty in the same year. Hu's participation in the quelling of the Man disturbance is mentioned only in his biography. The pacification was only temporarily effective, for the Man of this area periodically rebelled during the following years.

31. For this reorganization of the government, see Goodrich, p. 11, and Balazs, "Le traité économique," p. 211, n. 112.

32. Ch'ien-t'un Mountain is identified by Ku Tsu-yü 顧祖禹 with Chien-t'ou Mountain 汧頭山 or Chi-t'ou Mountain 笄頭山 (see Tu-shih fang-yü chi-yao 讀史方輿紀要, 58.6a-b). Chi-t'ou Mt. is west of modern P'ing-liang 平涼 in central Kansu. Ku (loc. cit.) attributed this identification to Tu Yu 杜佑; however, Ch'ien-t'un Mt. does not appear in the discussion of Chi-t'ou Mt. in T'ung-tien 173.918a. See also Tzu-chih t'ung-chien 166.28b. The mountain had often been used as a refuge. For example, Mo-ch'i Tao-lo 万俟道洛 was killed there by Erh-chu T'ien-kuang 爾朱天光 (WS 75.19b) and Hou-mo-ch'en Yüeh 侯莫陳悅 was beheaded there by Yü-wen Tao 宇文導 (CS 10.3a).

33. Ching Prefecture was the modern Ching-ch'uan 涇川 in eastern Kansu.

34. Yün-yang, near modern Ching-yang 涇陽 in Shensi, was due north of Ch'ang-an. Yü-wen T'ai died on November 21, 556 and was buried on January 29, 557 (CS 2.18a).

35. The heir of T'ai was Chüeh 覺, cognomen T'o-lo-ni 陀羅尼, Skt. Dhāranī, the third son of T'ai. His mother was the sister of Emperor Hsiao-wu 孝武 of the Wei. T'ai's first son was born of a commoner, and his second son was already dead. Chüeh, born in 542, was fourteen at this time. In 550 he had been enfeoffed as Duke of Lüeh-yang Commandery 略陽郡. In the early part of 556 he was made T'ai's heir. He inherited the titles of Grand Tutor and Chancellor on November 22, the day after his father's death. See his annals, CS 3.1a.

36. The meaning of the statement is not clear. It may perhaps refer to a pun on the homophony, but for tone, of the two words.

Again, the hu 胡 may have been associated with Yü-wen Hu because of his child-name Sa-pao, also the Chinese name of the headsman of Iranian communities in China. See note 1 above.

37.. The title of Pillar of State, established during the Warring States period, was given to a general who had won many victories. During the Chou this distinction was important enough to warrant a notice in the annals on its bestowal to someone. In 575 it was found necessary to create a new, more honorific title, the Senior Pillar of State (shang chu-kuo 上柱國). See CS 12.5b.

38. The last emperor of the Wei, known as Kung-ti 恭帝, was T'o-pa K'uo 拓跋廓. He ascended the throne in 554 and abdicated it on February 14, 557. He was then made Duke of Sung 宋公, as the last king of the Shang dynasty had been named. He died later in the same year. Yü-wen Chüeh 宇文覺, posthumously known as Emperor Hsiao-min 孝閔, now ascended the throne. See CS 3.2a.

39. The office of Great Constable was supposedly used in the time of Yao and Shun. During the ancient Chou, the man with this title was the head of the Office of Summer, in charge of military affairs. It was also used for a time in the Han, in place of the Grand Guardian (t'ai-wei 太尉). The holders of the posts of Great Constable and Great General were called the "Two Greats" during the period of the Northern and Southern Dynasties.

40. The dukedoms, modelled after those of the Chou dynasty, were distributed on March 1, 557. Li Pi 李弼 was made Duke of Chao 趙; Chao Kuei, Duke of Ch'u 楚; Tu-ku Hsin, Duke of Han 韓; Yü Chin, Duke of Yen 燕 and Hou-mo-ch'en Ch'ung

侯莫陳業, Duke of Liang 梁. Each received an appanage of 10,000 households. See CS 3.4a.

41. Tu-ku Hsin, a T'o-pa, also came from Wu-ch'uan. He took part in the battle with P'o-liu-han Pa-ling and was later captured by Ko Jung. He passed on to the army of Erh-chu Jung, and was assigned to Ho-pa Sheng 賀拔勝. Sheng sent him into Shensi when Sheng's brother Yüeh 岳 was killed, and there Hsin joined Yü-wen T'ai. Hsin was an excellent general, and his life for the most part was spent in a series of campaigns. He also had the distinction of being the father of three empresses, each of a different dynasty. His biography occurs in CS 16.3a-10a and PS 61.5a-8b.

42. Other men mentioned in an edict issued on April 2, 557, after the suppression of the plot, included Mo-ch'i Chi-t'ung 万侯懃通, Ch'ih-nu Hsing 叱奴興, Wang Lung-jen 王龍仁, and Chang-sun Seng-yen 長孫僧衍 (CS 3.4b). Ch'ih-nu Hsing, with the rank of Palatine, had taken part in a campaign in the northwest the previous year (CS 19.14b). Chang-sun Seng-yen was the eldest son of Chang-sun Chien 長孫儉 (PS 22.5a). None of these men have biographies in the standard histories. Because of the importance of Tu-ku Hsin, Hu wished to keep silent his part in the matter, and his name was not mentioned in the edict. This plot is discussed in the Introduction, p. 13.

43. See Chou li 1.1a-b.

44. Li Chih was the son of Li Yüan 李遠, a high-ranking official of the Chou. Yüan at this time held the rank of Pillar of State Great General and was stationed at Hung-nung. While Chih is here said to be General Accountant, an officer described in the Chou li (6.21b) as head of the department which kept the

accounts of the state, his own biography states that he was General Recorder and Consultant Officer (ssu-lu ts'an-chün 司錄參軍) of the chancellor's staff and in charge of the administration of the court (CS 25.13a).

45. Sun Heng has no biography in the standard histories.

46. I-fu Feng was the son of I-fu Lang 乙弗朗. Lang had lived in the T'ai Prefecture area, came south because of the disorders of the 520's and entered Erh-chu Jung's employ. He came to Ch'ang-an with the Wei emperor in 534 and was held in high esteem at the court. He died some time before this plot was formed. His biography is in PS 49.26a-b. Feng is only mentioned in his father's biography as being put to death for the plot against Hu.

The Majordomo, according to the Chou li (3.22b), was under the Office of Heaven. The duties of the officer with this title were to take charge of the court retainers and keep a list of their names. See also Sui shu 12.29a.

47. Chang Kuang-lo, Ho-pa T'i and Yüan Chin do not have biographies in the standard histories. For the first, see also note 50.

48. A passage very similar to this occurs in the Tso chuan, Duke Yin, 1st year (Legge, V, 2) in a somewhat analogous situation. The passage 不如早為之所，無使滋蔓，蔓難圖之 is translated (freely) by Legge (ibid., p. 5b), "You had better take the necessary precautions and not allow the danger to grow so great that it will be difficult to deal with it."

49. These are among the opening words of the Lo kao 洛誥 of the Shu ching (Legge, III, 434-436). As Legge points out, there has been some question as to the interpretation of this

passage, revolving about the meaning of fu 復. The pseudo-K'ung An-kuo 孔安國 commentary, followed by K'ung Ying-ta 孔穎達, interpreted the passage as meaning that the Duke of Chou was returning the government to his nephew, King Ch'eng 成王, when the latter reached maturity. Thus, fu was taken to mean fu huan... cheng 復還... 政 "to return the administration" (Shang shu 15.14b). In the Sung, the fu came to be interpreted as "report." Karlgren, in his article "Glosses on the Book of Documents, Part II," BMFEA, XXI (1949), 74, adduces evidence in the Shu ching and the Han shu in support of this view. Believing that this was the oldest interpretation, he therefore translates the passage as, "I report to (you) my son and bright sovereign."

That the first interpretation was more than a commentator's surmise is shown by the phrase Chou kung fan cheng 周公反政 in Shih chi 4.16a. The context of the situation shows that Feng and the others had this first interpretation in mind. The same chapter of the Shu ching concludes with the statement that the Duke of Chou had held the regency for seven years (Legge, III, 452; cf. Shih chi, loc. cit.).

50. According to the annals, Chang Kuang-lo disclosed the plot to Hu at this time. As he later served Hu in revealing further plans of the dissidents (see Translation, p. 51 above), he evidently was not himself suspected. See CS 3.6b. He is mentioned in 575 as taking part in the invasion of Ch'i with the rank of Great General (CS 30.11b).

51. Liang Prefecture comprised the area about Nan-cheng 南鄭 on the upper Han River (the Han-chung 漢中 region), while T'ung Prefecture was in the area of modern Mien-yang 緜陽 in

-Notes to pp. 35-36-

western Szechwan.

The title of tz'u-shih was given to the imperial envoy in each prefecture whose task it was to uncover any maladministration in the area under his jurisdiction. At this time, since he often was in charge of the troops of his prefecture, it may be assumed he also had administrative duties. See TT 32.184b. For a discussion of this office, see also Eberhard, Das Toba-Reich Nordchinas, pp. 97-103.

52. The Li Hsien 李賢 commentary (Hou-Han shu 後漢書 43.23b) explains the meaning of fu yü ch'un-ch'iu 富於春秋. Yen Chih-t'ui 顏之推 (sixth century A.D.) provides an illuminating comment, contemporary with our text, on misuse of the expression; see Yen-shih chia-hsün 顏氏家訓, Pao-ching-t'ang ts'ung-shu 抱經堂叢書 ed., 3.24b.

53. The altars of the soil and grain (she-chi 社稷), erected by every ruler, were typically represented as palladia on whose security the safety of the state depended. See the monograph by Chavannes, Le dieu du sol dans la Chine antique, appendix to Le T'ai chan (Paris, 1910), pp. 437-525.

54. Ho-lan Hsiang (515?-562?), cognomen Sheng-lo 盛樂, was a cousin of Hu, as his mother was a sister of Hu's father. He fought under T'ai's command in Shensi, and became known for his martial abilities. He was made Assistant Constable in 556, and Great Constable in 557, succeeding Hu in this post. He cooperated closely with Hu in establishing the dynasty and ousting Chao Kuei. His biography appears in CS 20.4b-9a and PS 61.17a-18b. The reading of his cognomen is made clear by the substitution of 洛 for 樂 in a later passage, CS 11.8a. His biography places his death in 564, while the annals give 562. Since he was

seventeen (sui) in 531, the latter date seems correct.

55. Yü-ch'ih Kang (517-569) bore the cognomen P'o-lo 婆羅 (Skt. Bāla). Through his mother he was a cousin of Hu. He fought under T'ai and gained the important post of Commander of the Palace Troops in 554. Following the present incident he was made Assistant Constable and Pillar of State. His biography appears in CS 20.9a-11b and PS 62.13b-16a.

According to Chou li 28.1b, there were two Assistant Constables under the Great Constable. During the Northern Chou, there seems to have been but one.

56. The palace troops were made up of contingents supplied by the regular armies. These soldiers were given this duty for a short period on a rotation basis. The general in charge of the guard had more permanent tenure. See PS 60.24a and 25a.

57. Ch'in lao 勤勞 occurs in the Shu ching, Chin t'eng 金縢 chapter (Legge, III, 360). The passage refers to the Duke of Chou and is rendered by Legge, "Formerly the duke was thus earnest for the royal House." This text has replaced chia 家 with yeh 業.

58. This was the title of Emperor Hsiao-min before his accession to the throne. Lüeh-yang still bears this name and is in southwestern Shensi.

59. The usual meaning of cheng ti 正嫡 is the legal wife in contrast to concubines. The heir is then known as ti tzu 嫡子. Another designation of the legal wife is cheng shih 正室; see K'ang-hsi tzu-tien. However, this last term is also used for the heir (Chou li 19.3b with commentary of Cheng Hsüan). It would seem that the twofold usage of cheng shih was extended also to cheng ti, but the meaning "heir" is comparatively rare.

-Notes to p. 37-

60. Shih ching, Po chou 柏舟 Ode (Legge, IV, 40). Cheng Hsüan interprets the words as "a group of men of low moral character (hsiao jen 小人) at the ruler's side" (Mao shih 2A. 7a).

61. Mien mu 面目 occurs in the Shih ching, Ho jen ssu 何人斯 Ode (Legge, IV, 346):

"But when one with face and eyes stands opposite to another,
The man can be seen through and through."

The words occur in the Shih chi (39.14b) in a context resembling the present case (Chavannes, Les mémoires historiques de Se-ma Ts'ien, IV, 279); cf. also Shih chi 7.34a (Chavannes, op. cit., II, 319). Almost these same words were used when Ho Kuang 霍光 deposed a son of Emperor Wu of the Han; see Han shu 68.6a.

62. Duke of Ning-tu was at this time the title of Yü-wen Yü 宇文毓, the eldest son of T'ai; see note 67. Ning-tu was near the modern Han-yin 漢陰 in Shensi. The title had previously been held by Yü-wen T'ai.

63. Kuei hsin 歸心, a popular phrase in these edicts, occurs in Analects 20.1 (Legge, I, 351). T'ien hsia chih min kuei hsin yen 天下之民歸心焉 is rendered by Legge as ". . . throughout the kingdom the hearts of the people turned towards him."

64. Chu i 注意, a verb-object construction like kuei hsin, occurs in the Shih chi (46.20b). It is translated by Chavannes (Mém. hist., V, 281) as "y appliquer sa réflexion."

65. This sentence occurs at least five times in the Tso chuan; see Hung, Combined Concordances to Ch'un-ch'iu, Kung-yang, Ku-liang and Tso-chuan. Harvard-Yenching Index Series, Supplement, Vol. XI, pt. 4, p. 239a, s.v. t'ing 聽. Legge varies his translation of the words to fit the various contexts. The ren-

dering chosen is that which appears in Legge, V, 409.

66. Emperor Hsiao-min died at the age of 16, sometime between November 1 and 4. Chih's father, Li Yüan 李遠, was forced to commit suicide on December 5 for daring to defend his son. See CS 4.1b.

67. Shih-tsung was the temple name of Yü-wen Yü 毓, who had the childhood name of T'ung-wan-t'u 統萬突, after the city T'ung-wan where he was born. The suffix -t'u appears in the cognomens of most of his brothers. He was the eldest son of T'ai and was born in 534, when T'ai was still in Hsia Prefecture. In 548 he was made Duke of Ning-tu Commandery. When Emperor Hsiao-min ascended the throne earlier in 557, Yü was made prefect of Ch'i Prefecture, just south of Feng-hsiang 鳳翔 in Shensi, about 80 miles west of Ch'ang-an.

68. This was on the first day of the first Chinese month (February 4, 558) (CS 4.2a).

69. The presentation of these objects by the emperor was an occasion of great importance. See also Sui shu 10.7b and 11.21b. Yü-ch'ih Chiung had been presented with similar clothing in 556 (CS 21.3b).

70. Yü-wen Chih, cognomen Ch'ien-fu 乾附, was the third son of Hu. He was later made the heir of P'u-t'i 菩提, the son of Yü-wen Lo-sheng 宇文洛生, both of whom were killed by Kao Huan. Chih was executed with his father and deprived of his titles. In 574 the titles were posthumously restored to him. See CS 10.9b and Translation, p. 62 above.

71. Warden was the title applied to the heads of provinces by the Chou li (2.14b). It was used occasionally in the Han and came to be restricted to Ch'ang-an. The change of nomenclature

-Notes to p. 38-

mentioned in the text followed this usage, as Yung Prefecture contained Ch'ang-an.

72. The title of the office was changed on March 4, 558, and the office given to Hu on May 9 (CS 4. 2b-3a).

73. Tso chuan, Duke Hsiang, 11th year (Legge, V, 450-451, tr. p. 453b), relates that the first occurrence of such a gift was that made by the Marquis of Chin to a loyal minister for his part in bringing about peace among the states.

74. The reign title was established on October 1, 559, the first to be announced for the new dynasty (CS 4. 7a). At the same time, the term for the emperor was changed from wang 王 to huang-ti 皇帝. Ch'en Yin-k'o, (op. cit., p. 93) points these out as violations of ancient Chou practices.

75. This was on February 13, 559 (CS 4. 4b).

76. Wang Ch'ang 王昶 included in his Chin-shih ts'ui-pien 金石萃編 (36.1a-b) the text of a Buddhist dedicatory inscription dated 560, which extends felicitous wishes to the Emperor and the Duke of Chin. Wang points out that the omission of Hu's name and his being ranked with the Emperor are indications of the power which he wielded at this time (ibid., 5a-b). The Hsü-hsiu Shan-hsi-sheng t'ung-chih kao 續修陝西省通志稿 (140.18b) states that this inscription is to be found in Hsien-yang 咸陽. Another notice of the same sort, dated 569, appears in Chin-shih ts'ui-pien 37.16a-b.

77. Li An was killed together with Hu in 572. He has no biography in the standard histories. See also p. 58 above.

78. This post was a minor one in the department which looked after the food and liquid refreshments for imperial feasts. See Hu San-hsing's 胡三省 commentary, TCTC 168, p. 5204 (Peking

ed., 1959), first year of t'ien-chia 天嘉, fourth month.

79. Shih-tsung died on May 30, 560, at the age of 26. His posthumous name was Emperor Ming-huang 明皇. He had been well taught and had supported many scholars at his court. In an edict issued just before his death, he stated that death was one of the certainties of life, so there should be no regret. He called on the others to rally to the aid of his worthy elder brother (sic) Hu and not to forget T'ai's wishes. Because of the youth of his own child, he appointed his younger brother Yung as heir. See CS 4.8a-10a.

80. Kao-tsu was the temple name of Yü-wen Yung 宇文邕 (543-578), cognomen Ni-lo-t'u 禰羅突, the fourth son of T'ai. (Note the variant Mi-lo-t'u 彌羅突 recorded by Hu San-hsing, TCTC 168, p. 5205, first year of t'ien-chia, fourth month.) In 558 he entered the court to become Grand Minister of Public Works (ta ssu-k'ung 大司空) and Duke of Lu 魯公. He was made emperor on May 31, 560. See CS 5.1b.

81. This sentence occurs in the Shu ching (Legge, III, 191) and in Analects 14.43 (Legge, I, 291).

82. This reign title was established on the first day of the Chinese year (February 1, 561). It was to last until 565.

83. This took place on February 1, 561. The system of government of the Chou had six independent offices; see n. 31 above. Five of these were now placed under the direct control of the Office of Heaven (t'ien-kuan 天官) whose head, of course, was Hu. See also CS 5.2a.

84. T'ung Prefecture was the modern Ta-li 大荔, northeast of Ch'ang-an. See Goodrich, p. 101, n. 235. Two emperors, Yü-wen Chüeh and Yü-wen Yung, were born there. It

-Notes to pp. 9-40-

seems to have been a subsidiary capital of the Western Wei and Chou. See Tzŭ-chih t'ung-chien 166.28b. Hsia-yang 夏陽, in this prefecture had armories and military colonies (CS 35.21b). See also Balazs, "Le traité économique," p. 275.

85. The two clauses here predicated of Yü-wen Hu occur in the I ching (7.Da). The third century commentator Wang Pi 王弼 makes the second clause dependent on the first.

86. The distinction of forbidding the use of the given name (ming 名) in various official documents was one of three special privileges which had been closely associated with one another since the second century A.D. (The other two were permission to enter the court wearing a sword and to refrain from hurrying when entering the court.) Since the granting of these privileges to Ts'ao Ts'ao 曹操 in A.D. 212, they had been typically sought by would-be usrpers. See discussion in Miyakawa Hisayuki 宮川尚之, Zejo ni yoru ōchō kakumei no tokushitsu 禪讓による王朝革命の特質, Tōhōgaku, XI (1955), 50-58 (see esp. p. 53), and sources cited in the same author's Rikuchōshi kenkyū 六朝史研究 (Tokyo, 1956), p. 99, n. 3. The terminology in the present case departs somewhat from the usual formula, which distinguishes it from the cases of the usurpers.

87. More literally, "to effect seizure by the horns and the legs," as in catching a deer. The figure was originally used, in less terse form, of the joint strategy of the state of Chin and the Jung barbarians; see Tso chuan 32.13a, with K'ung Ying-ta's comment.

88. The Kao family ruled the state of Ch'i to the east of Chou. On the ascendancy of this family and the earlier conflicts between Eastern and Western Wei, see Introduction, pp. 6-7 above.

At this time the reigning sovereign was Kao Chan 高湛, posthumously known as Emperor Wu-ch'eng 武成, the ninth son of Kao Huan.

89. Yang Chung (507-568), cognomen Yen-yü 檐于, was under the command of Tu-ku Hsin when the latter joined Yü-wen T'ai (see n. 41 above). Chung rose to high office because of his outstanding bravery in battle. In the discussion about the campaign, the men of the court said that the size of Ch'i required the use of at least 100,000 men. Chung insisted he would need only 10,000. See CS 19.16a-21a. His cognomen is the only transcription in the Chou shu identified as a word of the northern peoples. Its meaning is given as "fierce animal," quite possibly referring to hu 虎 'tiger,' which was a T'ang taboo. The writer is unable to identify it.

90. One of the dangers which Ch'i faced was the constant raids of the Juan-juan and other northern tribes. To guard against this, Kao Huan in 543 built a wall between the site of modern Ching-lo 靜樂 in the Fen River valley east to Kuo Prefecture 崞州 in the Hu-t'o 滹沱 River valley in northern Shansi (PCS 2.13a). Over a number of years his successor, Kao Yang 高洋, extended the system of walls and fortifications. These are described and located in Franke, II, 239-240 and III, 313-314. The wall from Ta-t'ung in Shansi east to the sea seems to have coincided to a large extent with the course of the extant Great Wall. West of Ta-t'ung it turned south and met the Yellow River west of Fen Prefecture. As Franke points out (II, 239-240), the walls, built at great expense, were not of much value to Ch'i, since there was greater danger from the south of the wall than there was from north of it.

-Notes to p. 40-

91. Yang Chung had great success at first. He crushed all opposition and soon came to Ping Prefecture 并州, the modern T'ai-yüan in Shansi. The T'u-chüeh under Mu-han 木汗 Qaghan also appeared before the city at this time with 100,000 men. Ta-hsi Wu 達奚武 was supposed to come up the Fen River with 30,000 troops, but he failed to appear. A great snowstorm disheartened the T'u-chüeh and they refused to fight. Chung lost the battle with the Ch'i forces in late January and early February of 564, but the victors were afraid to seize the initiative. The T'u-chüeh then plundered the countryside and left. Chung could only retreat back to the Chou capital, where he was received with enthusiasm. See CS 19. 21a-b, 5. 7b and 50. 6b. Note that this campaign ended early in 564, contrary to the implication of the present text.

The T'u-chüeh appeared at the court in the new year and requested that another expedition be sent against Ch'i. Ch'i had suffered great losses and had shown little resistance to the combined forces of Chou and the T'u-chüeh. Therefore the project was looked upon with favor, and on August 23, 564, Yang Chung was ordered to lead troops on another campaign. See CS 5. 8b, 19. 22a-b and 50. 7a. Material dealing with Northern Chou-T'u-chüeh relations, including these campaigns, is translated by Liu Mau-tsai, Die chinesischen Nachrichten zur Geschichte des Ost-Türken (T'u-küe); see pp. 11-27, passim.

92. While Hu and other members of the family had gone to Shensi, some had remained behind in the east and had fallen prisoner to Kao Huan. A few of these, including P'u-t'i 菩提, Kuang-pao 光寶 and Shih-fei 什肥, had been put to death by Kao

Huan. See CS 10.1b, 8b and 9b. The rest, all women and children, had been allowed to live.

93. About this time, Wei Hsiao-k'uan 韋孝寬 was made prefect of the newly-won prefecture of Hsün 勳, at modern Chi-shan 稷山 in southwestern Shensi. It is said that the state of Ch'i sent some men requesting permission to carry on trade. As there had been no peaceful intercourse between the two states for many years, this created some excitement. Hu sent an official from the capital with instructions to question the envoys about the members of his family held captive by Ch'i. In addition, Hsiao-k'uan sent back some men of Ch'i captured by the T'u-chüeh with a letter setting forth the good intentions of the Chou court. It was through this channel that the subsequent diplomatic intercourse took place. See CS 31.5a-b; PS 64.4a has the same material. See also Liu, Nachrichten, pp. 24 and 511-512 on the return by Ch'i of the hostages.

94. A translation of this letter, differing in some details from this version, appears in Sié Kang, L'amour maternel dans la littérature feminine en Chine (Paris, 1937), pp. 60-62. The letter has also been reproduced in numerous works concerning women's place in literature; see, e.g., punctuated text in Chung-kuo fu-nü wen-hsüeh-shih 中國婦女文學史, compiled by Hsieh Wu-liang 謝无量 (Shanghai, 1926), Pt. II, Sec. 2, pp. 93-94.

95. Yü-wen Hu left his mother in 531, according to our text (Translation, p. 30 above). As the letter was written in 564, the period of separation was actually 33 years.

96. The three boys were Shih-fei, Tao, and Hu. The Pei shih text (57.6a) says there were two girls. The only sister of

Hu about whom I have information is the one given in marriage to Ch'ih-lieh-fu Kuei 叱列伏龜 in 537 (CS 20.12a).

97. Aunt Yang was an elder sister of Yü-wen T'ai. Yen-shih chia-hsün, 2.6a, states that married paternal aunts are referred to by their husband's surnames. Other elder sisters of Yü-wen T'ai are mentioned in CS 20.4a, 20.8b, 21.1a and perhaps 33.2b.

98. Ho-kan must refer to the wife of Lo-sheng 洛生, Yü-wen T'ai's brother, who was of this clan (see the Genealogical Table). All editions of the Chou shu consulted substitute yü 于 for the kan 干 of the Pei shih. However, the occurrence of Ho-kan in CS 27.14b and WS 113.42b substantiates the Pei shih reading. The "bride" was most probably the wife of Shih-fei, who had elected to remain behind with his mother and was soon killed. Her son Chou 胄 later came back from Ch'i to Chou; see n. 29 above.

99. Po-ling Commandery was at modern An-p'ing 安平 in Hopei. Tso-jen City was over 100 miles northwest of this, near the modern T'ang District 唐縣. The course of the T'ang River passed halfway between Po-ling and Tso-jen. Ting Prefecture was at modern Ting District, on the T'ang River. The party had to bypass this prefecture to reach their destination.

100. The Lady Ho-pa was the wife of Lien 連, a brother of Yü-wen T'ai. Kuang-pao 光寶 is mentioned briefly in the biography of his father (CS 10.8b and PS 57.12a) as having been killed by Kao Huan. The Chou shu gives his name there as Kuang-pao, while the Pei shih has Yüan-pao. Other editions of the Chou shu for this text also have Yüan, perhaps due to assimilation with the name of Yüan Pao-chang (see n. 101 below). For the Lady Ho-kan, see note 98 above. For P'u-t'i (Skt. bodhi),

PS 57.13a has P'u-sa 菩薩 (Bodhisattva).

101. Yüan Li 元麗, cognomen Pao-chang, was the grandson of Yüan Huang 元晃, who was posthumously made an emperor of the Wei. Li was very active in keeping western China under the control of the Wei and earned a reputation of being harsh in his administration. He was made prefect of Chi Prefecture 冀州 in northern China for a time, but unfortunately nothing is said of this period except that he had two hundred Taoists killed. When the emperor later asked him about this, he replied that two hundred dead Taoists could hardly be considered a great number. The emperor was enraged by his flippant answer, and he was tried for the crime. While no mention is made of the verdict, the next remark is that his posthumous name was Wei 威, "Severe." See WS 19A.11a-12a.

102. PS 57.6b has ch'ien 千, "thousand" for shih 十, "ten." T'ang City was one of seven districts under the jurisdiction of Chungshan Commandery 中山郡 (WS 106A.7b-8a). The population of the commandery as a whole was given as 255,241 persons in 532-534 (WS 106A.1b-2a and 7b). If the figures have any validity, and assuming an equal division among the seven, the area under the jurisdiction of T'ang City could have had approximately 36,000 persons. It would therefore be possible that six or seven thousand were made captive, but it is hardly probable.

103. Chi K'u-ken has no biography in the standard histories.

104. The Ju-ju, also known under the names Jou-jan 柔然 and Juan-juan 蠕蠕, were the Altaic tribe then leading the confederation of northern nomads. See Chavannes, Documents sur les T'ou-kiue occidentaux, pp. 229-233; for a suggestion as to the etymology of the name, see P. A. Boodberg, Sino-Altaica,

-Notes to p. 43-

III, Pt. 1: "Avars and Kermikhiōns," Berkeley, 1935 (photographic reproduction of manuscript). See further references in R. A. Miller, Accounts of the Western Nations in the History of the Northern Chou Dynasty (Berkeley, 1959), p. 19, n. 11.

105. The Pei shih text (57.7a) reads 壽 instead of 受. During this period there were the similar place-names Shou-yang 受陽 and Shou-yang City 壽陽城, both listed as parts of T'ai-yüan Commandery 太原郡 (WS 106A.11b-12a). The seat of this commandery was located in Chin-yang District 晉陽縣, which is twice mentioned as the place from which Yü-wen Hu departed for the west (CS 11.1a and 20.4b). The more immediate relation of Shou-yang 受陽 to Chin-yang (see WS 106A.12a) and the earlier date of the Chou shu text suggest that this is the place intended.

106. Sheng-lo was the cognomen of Ho-lan Hsiang; see n. 54 above. He was orphaned in 525 (or 527) at the age of eleven sui (CS 20.4b). His biography also says that he was in Chin-yang with Hu when they were summoned westward in 531.

107. For this portion of the text, the Pei shih account (57.8a) seems better. The ling 淩 of the Chou shu is replaced by ju 汝 'you' which is necessary before the next word, teng 等. Also, the Chou shu text has reversed the order of ju 汝 and kung 共 in referring to the aunts, which can make no sense.

108. Erh-chu Jung was given the title of Pillar of Heaven on August 12, 529 (WS 10.12a). In his biography (WS 74.15a) the date is given as 530. The edict granting it said it was being used for the first time. Jung was killed in 530.

109. Ho-pa A-tou-ni was Ho-pa Yüeh; see n. 10 above.

110. While the pass is usually identified as that of Han-ku, at

this period Tʻung Pass seems to have been considered the dividing point between the two states.

111. The third member of the party is unknown.

112. A-ma-tun may have been the Hsien-pei word for 'mother.' See Shiratori, p. 88 and Boodberg, "The Language of the Tʻo-pa Wei," HJAS, I (1936), 170.

113. For this phrase, see Tso chuan, Duke Hsiang, 24th year (Legge, V, 505).

114. More literally, "wearing heaven on the head and treading on the earth." For the first phrase see Li chi 3.10b. The whole expression occurs, e.g., in the Wu-Yüeh chʻun-chʻiu 吳越春秋(SPTK ed.) 3.6a.

115. This statement is borne out by CS 46.7b-8b, which tells of Hu's interest in and solicitude for Ching Kʻo 荆可, who attracted notice by his filial actions in his mother's behalf. The explanation of Hu's interest in Kʻo emphasizes Hu's feelings of guilt at not being able to carry out his own duties as a filial son.

116. For hsi hsia 膝下 see Hsiao ching 5.4b. The phrase refers to the time spent under the care of one's parents.

117. Wang lo 囲羅, literally "nets and snares," was sometimes used figuratively of legal punishments, especially where undeserved or unduly harsh. See, e.g., Wei Yüan Shao hsi Yü-chou 為袁紹檄豫州 by Chʻen Lin 陳琳 (d. A.D. 217), Liu-chʻen-chu Wen-hsüan 44.10b. In the present case retribution by Heaven is probably implied.

118. The Shih ching, Yü wu cheng 雨無正 ode (Legge, IV, 328), has the words chʻi hsüeh 泣血, "I wept blood." The Han-fei tzu 韓非子 (SPTK ed., 4.6b) tells of a man who wept for three days and three nights. When his tears were exhausted,

he chi chih i hsüeh 繼之以血 "continued them with blood" as in our text.

119. Note that the expression te yin 德音, "virtuous words," was used of a class of writing devoted to the words of emperors. See E. D. Edwards, "A Classified Guide to the Thirteen Classes of Chinese Prose," BSOAS, XII (1947-48), 779; also Tz'u hai, s.v., definition two.

120. Ma-tun 麿敦 is of course a contraction of a-ma-tun, on which see n. 112 above.

121. On Ho-tung see n. 26 above.

122. Erh ya 7.1a describes Chi Province 冀州, one of the ancient nine, as being between two rivers. The two rivers are explained by Kuo P'u 郭璞 as being the East and West Rivers, actually the Yellow River in both cases. The "Land between the Rivers" is an allusion to Ch'i, as ancient Chi formed a large part of Ch'i, including the capital.

123. The "Three Props" (san fu 三輔) was an expression used, since the second century B.C., to refer to Ch'ang-an and two neighboring cities; hence it came to stand, by extension, for this region in Central Shensi. See Dubs, History of the Former Han Dynasty, II, 113 and 158; also Chin shu 56.1b. It is here appropriately used to indicate the seat of the Northern Chou.

124. Sheng hsia 升遐, "to ascend afar," was a figure used of the death of emperors; see Dai kanwa jiten 1617c, definition two, for early instances and variants. On "making certain the Heavenly Protection" (t'ien-pao 天保) see the T'ien pao ode (Legge, IV, 255-258).

125. N.b. passages in the Tso chuan, Legge, V, 494 (tr. p. 496b) and 706 (tr. p. 711a).

126. On this robe see the text of Hu's mother's letter, p. 43 above.

127. Note the function of the form i 移 as set forth by Liu Hsieh (ca. 465-522), and of the hsi 檄 with which it is closely associated (Wen-hsin tiao-lung 文心彫龍, SPTK ed., 4.12a-14a; tr. by Vincent Y.-C. Shih, The Literary Mind and the Carving of Dragons, New York, 1959, pp. 117-121).

128. Analects, 12.7; Legge, I, 254.

129. In Analects, 12.7, Confucius listed the three necessities of government in their order of importance as confidence in the ruler, adequate food, and last of all adequate arms (Legge, I, 254).

130. Ch'ung-erh was the Duke Wen of Chin 晉文公, one of the pa 霸 or hegemons of the Chou. His life is treated in the Shih chi, 39.5a-27a and passim in the Tso chuan. According to Chavannes (Mémoires historiques, IV, 291-308) the dates of his rule over Chin were 636-628 B.C. According to the Tso chuan, Duke Hsi, 26th year (Legge, V, 194, tr. p. 196b), Ch'ung-erh, while besieging a city, supplied his troops with rations for three days and vowed that if the city had not fallen within that time, he would withdraw. The city did not fall and he left, although his spies assured him that the city would surrender the next evening. He said he did this because if he took the city against his word, his loss would be greater than his gain.

131. Sui Hui was a man of Chin who served as a minister first of Ch'in 秦 and later of his native state. It was said of him, "The affairs of his family were well regulated, in conversing (with his ruler) about the State, he concealed nothing, his officers of prayers set forth the truth before the Spirits, and used

-Notes to p. 49-

no speeches he could be ashamed of." See Tso chuan, Duke Hsiang, 27th year (Legge, V, 530, tr. p. 533b). Sui Hui is known by many names in the Tso; see Hung, Concordances to Ch'un-ch'iu, II, 262b, s.v. Shih Hui 士會 .

132. The idiom is literally "to eat one's words." This differs from the English idiom, which implies retraction of a statement under coercion. These words occur in the Shu. As K'ung Ying-ta mentions, some commentators and glosses, the Erh ya among them, have equated shih 食 with wei 偽 . However, he explains the idiom by saying, ". . . speaking and not carrying out [the import of the words] is like eating them down to nothing. One is false (wei 偽) if in one's actions one does not follow the words previously spoken. Therefore it is universally said that [to speak] 'false words' is 'to eat one's words.' For this reason the Erh ya glosses shih 食 as wei 偽 ." See Shu-ching 8. 2b and 4a.

133. These are two hexagrams of the I ching. The first (Chou i 1. 28a) is interpreted as "The strong and weak begin to mingle and difficulties arise." The second (ibid., 4. 13b) is explained as "Brightness entering the earth and brightness is injured." In another place (ibid., 9.13b) i 夷 is equated with shang 傷 "to injure." I have been unable to determine whether the correlation of hexagrams with time represented a fixed mechanical correspondence with certain units of the time sequence or was applied more freely in a descriptive manner.

134. San chi 三紀 occurs in Shu-ching 19. 6b. Chi is here defined as being twelve years, the duration of Jupiter's orbit.

135. Ku 姑 is defined in the Erh ya (4.14b) as being the sister of one's father. The person in question here was Lady Yang,

Yü-wen T'ai's sister. Shih mu 世母 is explained as the wife of an older brother of one's father (ibid., 4.15b). This was the relationship of Madame Yen to the emperor.

136. These words seem to be derived from the Tso chuan, Duke Yin, 3rd year (Legge, V, 11, tr. p. 13a). There the phrase occurs in the negative form, and the words following are also significant: "If there be not good faith in the heart, hostages are of no use."

137. Before Ch'ung-erh gained the throne of Chin, he was a fugitive in Ch'u 楚. The ruler of Ch'u asked him what was to be the reward for his kind treatment. Ch'ung-erh replied, "Women, gems and silks, your lordship has... What then should I have with which to recompense your kindness?" (Tso chuan, Duke Hsi, 23rd year; see Legge, V, 185, tr. p. 187b). In the corresponding passage of the Kuo yü 國語 (SPTK ed., 10.8a) the third century commentator Wei Chao 韋昭 glosses tzu nü 子女 as "beautiful women." For further ancient examples of the expression with this sense see Dai kanwa jiten, 3067a.

138. Different virtues are called "the constants of Heaven" (t'ien ching 天經) in different sources. See, e.g., Hsiao ching 3.3b-4a (filial piety) and Legge, V, 704 (tr. p. 708b) (li 禮, ritual decorum).

139. This is to say that the royal family of Chou is more than a mere private family; it is rather the recipient of the entire state bequeathed by Yü-wen T'ai. Therefore, although this matter concerned a relative, considerations of state had to be kept in mind. It would not be enough to gain a reputation for filial piety at the expense of realistic national considerations.

140. Mencius speaks of King T'ai who was constantly attacked

-Notes to p. 50- -93-

by the barbarians desirous of his land. Since a ruler should not injure his people with that by which he nourishes them, he left the country. The people, calling him a benevolent man, flocked after him. See Legge, II, 176.

141. The state of Cheng is reported in the Tso chuan, Duke Chao, 6th year, as casting its laws in metal so that all might see them. A worthy of the time sent a letter to the ruler saying that if the people knew the grounds of contention they would cast away propriety and "contend about a matter as small as the point of an awl or a knife." See Legge, V, 607, tr. p. 609a-b.

142. Ch'ang-p'ing was a city of Chao 趙 during the Warring States Period. In 260 B.C. a general of Ch'in captured and slaughtered a Chao army of 400,000 men at this place (Shih chi 43.38b; Chavannes, V, 119). The Shih chi (81.7a) tells about another occasion on which an army of Ch'in approached a city of Chao and states that the sounds of the war drums spurring on the soldiers to attack shook the tiles of the houses in the city.

143. Han-ku, near the modern Ling-pao 靈寶 in Honan, was an important pass dividing the territory of Han 韓 and Ch'in in the Warring States Period. The only mention of the pass in the chapters devoted to these states in the Shih chi refers to a victory of Han over Ch'in, which is hardly to the point. This battle must refer to one of the many victories of Ch'in over Han that led to the complete destruction of Han in 230 B.C. (Chavannes, V, 222).

144. Both of these examples concern Ch'in in its relations with the neighboring states to the east. As Ch'in occupied the same geographical area as Northern Chou, the examples were very pointed.

145. It is unclear in what manner "swallowing blood 抔血" expresses grief. The words are used to express the conditions of life of primitive peoples (Li chi 21.11a-b). The more usual expression is "to weep tears of blood" (see n. 118). Perhaps the tears of blood were copious enough to drink.

146. Both of these are examples of filial piety and the close relationship between mother and son. The first occurs in Hou-Han shu 39.21a. It tells of a man out gathering wood who dropped everything and ran home when his mother, wishing to summon him, bit her finger. The second example refers to a story in the Chan kuo ts'e 戰國策 (SPTK ed., 4.51b). A mother tells her son that when he leaves on a mission, she leans on the doorpost looking for his return.

147. A direct quotation of a passage from the Tso chuan already alluded to above; see n. 87.

148. As mentioned above (n. 137), Ch'ung-erh (Duke Wen of Chin) was once asked by the ruler of Ch'u for a promise of compensation. When pressed for an answer, Ch'ung-erh frankly said that should Ch'u and Chin ever go to war and the ruler of Ch'u send no command to cease hostilities, he would take his weapons in hand and "maneuver with your lordship" (Legge, V, 185, tr. p. 187b).

149. N.b. Hsiao ching 1.4b: "He who loves his parents does not dare to be hateful toward other men. He who respects his parents does not dare to be disrespectful toward other men." Our text in effect uses the attribute of the first case with the result stated in the second case.

150. Ni-fu 尼父 (also written 尼甫) was a respectful epithet of Confucius, presumably based on his cognomen Chung-ni 仲尼.

-Notes to p. 52-

For explanations of ni see Chavannes, Mém. hist., V, 288-291, fn., and T. S. Tjan, Po Hu T'ung (2 vols., Leiden, 1949-52), pp. 113, fn. and 533, fn.

151. The Mencius (Legge, II, 303-304) contains the statement that two elder worthies of the time of King Wen, hearing that he knew well how to nourish the aged, went to offer their services to him.

152. The jade ring with a hiatus (chüeh 玦) and the complete ring (huan 環) are said to have been presented in antiquity to guilty persons to signify respectively banishment to the frontier and return from banishment. See Hsün tzu 荀子 (SPTK ed.) 19.2b, with commentary of Yang Liang.

153. This was in the ninth month of 564 (September 21 to October 20), thirty-three years after Hu had left her (CS 5.8b). Pei Ch'i shu 16.6b-7a says that Tuan Shao 段韶, who was at the northern border to stave off the attacks of the T'u-chüeh, advised that permission for her return be granted but that she not be sent until the Chou state gave proof of their desire for peaceful relations. His counsel was not heeded, and the attack on Ch'i followed her return. Pei shih 54.18a-b gives the same account in abbreviated form.

154. Fu 伏 and la 臘 designated certain special sacrifices in antiquity. See, on the former, Chavannes, Mém. hist., II, 23 and B. Schindler, "On the Travel, Wayside and Wind Offerings in Ancient China," Asia Major, I (1924), 652-656. By the third century B.C. the la sacrifice had been established as a part of the observance of the winter solstice, to judge by the Yüeh ling 月令 (Couvreur, Li ki, I, 396, with fn.); and the fu came to serve as its mid-summer counterpart. By the first century

B.C. the recurring phrases sui-shih fu-la 歲時伏臘 (and ssu-shih fu-la 四時伏臘, as here) suggest that equinoctial observances had become associated with these solstitial rites. See Han shu 66.14a; the same text appears in Wen hsüan 41.29b. The la rite in particular had been an expression, from Later Han times, of regard and care for aged parents; see examples discussed by Moriya Mitsuo 守屋美都雄 in [Kō-chū] Kei-So saijiki [校註] 荊楚歲時記 (Tokyo, 1950), pp. 191-192. (On the fu, see ibid., pp. 144-145.) This association also appears in sixth century texts for the ssu-shih fu-la, especially in relation to mourning for deceased parents; see, e.g., Ch'en shu 32.4a and Yen-shih chia-hsün 顏氏家訓 (Pao-ching-t'ang ts'ung-shu 抱經堂叢書 ed.) 2.15a. Another contemporary text speaks of an official who allowed prisoners to return to their homes for the fu and la observances; again the familial element is apparent. See Liang shu 51.6b. This practice had occurred as early as the first century A.D. See Hou Han shu 63.15b.

155. On this joint campaign with the T'u-chüeh see Introduction, pp. 15-17 above.

156. This refers to Huang-ti 黃帝. His ming 名 is said to have been Hsüan-yüan 軒轅. Only after three battles was he victorious over the descendants of Yen-ti 炎帝. See Shih chi 1.2a and 3b.

157. Chi Wu is Wu-wang of the Chou dynasty. On Chi as the surname of the Chou rulers see Shih chi 4.1b. The battle referred to resulted in the destruction of the army of the Shang. It is described in detail in the Wu-ch'eng 武成 chapter of the Shu ching (Legge, III, 306 ff.). (Note, however, that the present text by this name is not a genuine early portion of the Shu.)

158. The I ching reports that the people during the time of the mythical emperors fashioned bows and arrows, and these served to produce a feeling of awe everywhere (See Chou i 8. 7a). "The use of shields and dagger-axes" is probably a reference to the description of Huang-ti's chastisement of recalcitrant vassals in one of the three battles mentioned above (n. 156). See Shih chi 1. 2b.

In the Hou Han shu (13. 27a) a speaker refers to arms as "the great implements of emperors and kings" (ti wang chih ta ch'i 帝王之大器), virtually as in the present passage. The argument is the same, i.e., that arms cannot be dispensed with.

159. Shui neng ch'ü ping 誰能去兵 is taken from Tso chuan, Duke Hsiang, 27th year (Legge, V, 531, tr. p. 534a). The reason for maintaining arms, according to this text, is that "by them... the lawless are kept in awe, and accomplished virtue is displayed."

160. The first clause occurs in the Chung yung 中庸 (Legge, I, 429), where it is used in connection with Confucius. The second is found in the Shu ching, Wen hou chih ming 文侯之命 (Legge, III, 613).

161. This description of the founding of the Ch'i state is couched in language reserved for bandits and rebels. Ping and Chi were ancient names for the area included in the Ch'i state.

162. The Shu ching, T'ai shih 泰誓 (Legge, III, 290), has the words hui te chang wen 穢德彰聞, "The odor of such a state is plainly felt on high." Hui te is elaborated (Legge, loc. cit., fn.) as "their filthy, foetid deeds." (It may be noted that this chapter of the Shu is not one of the authentic early chapters.) In the Chiu kao 酒誥 (Legge, III, 409) there occur the words hsing wen

tsai shang 腥聞在上, "The rank odor... went loudly up on high." These passages both have to do with evil conditions on earth. The present text has combined the two to read hsing hui chang wen 腥穢彰聞.

This passage is perhaps partially explained by the Tso chuan, Duke Huan, 6th year (Legge, V, 47; tr. p. 49a). There it states that the ancient kings, in presenting their distilled and sweet spirits in the sacrifices, announced them as admirable and good, meaning that there was harmony in the land. They could then term their offerings fragrant. K'ung Ying-ta adds that if the people were not harmonious, then the wine and food of the offerings would stink and smell (hsing hui 腥穢; see Tso chuan 6.19b). The "rank odor" that "went on high" was then the odor of the sacrificial offerings, turned rancid by evil conditions on earth.

163. The Fen River flows south through central Shansi into the Yellow River. The Chin is a short stream, south of T'ai-yüan, which flows into the Fen. A clearer usage of these rivers to refer to the state to the east of the Northern Chou occurs in CS 27.20a.

164. Chi-meng was the cognomen of Wei Ao 隗囂. The Po-na text (Hou Han shu 13.1a) is probably in error in giving Chi-hsia 季夏. All other editions consulted give Chi-meng, including the Jen-shou 仁壽 edition of the Erh-shih-wu shih 二十五史 (Taipei, 1955-56), which reproduces a Southern Sung reprint of a Northern Sung text. Wei Ao nominally served Wang Mang, the Keng-shih 更始 Emperor, and finally Kung-sun Shu 公孫述; however, during most of this time (A.D. 23-33) he was de facto ruler of Kansu. Although he died before a decisive encounter

-Notes to p. 53- -99-

with the future Emperor Kuang-wu, his defeat was at least likely. See Hans Bielenstein, "The Restoration of the Han Dynasty," vol. II, BMFEA, XXXI (Stockholm, 1959), 1-280, especially pp. 24-26 and 184-187.

165. Po-kuei was the cognomen of Kung-sun Tsan 公孫瓚, a powerful leader in the extreme northeast during the chaotic period 180-200; see Hou Han shu 73.6b. For the phrase jih ts'u 日蹙 see Legge, IV, 567. The expression was used in the Shao min 召旻 ode to refer to the contraction of the Chou empire, and it was applied to the forces of Kung-sun Tsan with the same sense when he was under attack by Yüan Shao 袁紹 in A.D. 198 (Hou Han shu 73.14b).

166. Pi ching 彼境, more literally, "their borders," which, however, creates obvious ambiguities in English.

167. Yeh was the capital of Ch'i and was a short distance west of the modern Lin-chang 臨漳 in northern Honan. Ping Prefecture, or rather its administrative center Chin-yang, had been the seat of the Erh-chu (see n. 7 above). The Kao family continued this practice, making Chin-yang a secondary capital. See Tu-shih fang-yü chi-yao 4.29b-30b and 40.2a-b.

168. I refers to I Yin 伊尹, the assistant of T'ang 湯, the founder of the Shang dynasty. He is mentioned in Shih chi 3.2b and Mencius discussed him at length (Legge, II, 361 ff.). He supposedly wrote the chapter of the Shu entitled "The Counsels of I" (I hsün 伊訓); the extant text of this chapter, however, is not an authentic early document. See Legge, III, 191.

Lü refers to Lü Shang 呂尚, who assisted Kings Wen and Wu of the Chou. See Shih chi 32.1a-4a; Chavannes, Mém. hist., IV, 34-40.

169. For the twenty-four armies, see Introduction, p. 10 above.

170. These were probably the palace guards. See des Rotours, pp. 840 and 849.

171. Ch'in and Lung were the main part of the State, the area first occupied by the armies of Yü-wen T'ai; in a general way these names referred to Shensi and Kansu respectively. Pa and Shu (conquered in 553), the area lying to the west and southwest, were only added to the state later.

172. This was on November 28, 564 (CS 5.9a).

173. Yü-ch'ih Chiung, cognomen Po-chü-lo 薄居羅 (Skt. Vakula?), was a cousin of Yü-wen Hu, as his mother was a sister of T'ai. His brother Kang has been mentioned previously (see n. 55 above). Chiung's biography appears in CS 21.1a-5b and PS 62.9a-13b.

174. Ch'üan Ching-hsüan, cognomen Hui-yüan 揮遠, was a man from "west of the passes," unlike most of the other Chou generals. Some twenty years earlier he had fought in the area of Yü Prefecture, modern Ju-nan 汝南 in Honan. His biography is in CS 28.17b-21a and PS 61.26a-29b.

175. Shan-nan at this period seems to have referred to the upper Han River valley, extending down river at least as far as An-k'ang in Shensi; this may be inferred from cases of Shan-nan in CS 44.7b, 8a and 8b, and CS 33.16a. The name may also have been used to include the lower valley of the Han, as well as the territory about Chiang-ling 江陵; note that Ch'üan Ching-hsüan at this time was stationed at Chiang-ling and in charge of the defense of this area (CS 28.20a).

Shan-nan occurs again as Shan-nan Circuit 山南道, with

headquarters in Ching Prefecture 荊州 (modern Teng 鄧, S.W. Honan); see CS 19.8a. However, the same region is elsewhere called Tung-nan Circuit 東南道 (CS 6:1b and 26.1b). This suggests that in the present case "Tung-nan" may have been mistakenly changed to "Shan-nan" during the T'ang because of the use of "Shan-nan Circuit" for this area under that dynasty.

176. Yang Piao, cognomen Hsien-chin 顯進, was from central Shansi. His success against the Ch'i had brought him a fearsome reputation. His biography is in CS 34.4b-8b and PS 69.18a-20b.

177. Chih Pass is in Honan, some miles north of Lo-yang, across the Yellow River.

178. Yü-wen Hsien (544-578), cognomen P'i-ho-t'u 吡賀突, was the fifth son of T'ai. In 559 he was made Duke of Ch'i and in 564 he came to the capital as the Pastor of Yung Prefecture. He was put to death by his nephew, Hsüan-ti, in 578. His biography is in CS 12.1a-13a and PS 58.2a-8a. The text has dropped the name of his dukedom here, but it appears in other editions.

179. Ta-hsi Wu (504-570), cognomen Ch'eng-hsing 成興, was a T'o-pa from the native place of the Yü-wen and had entered Shensi in Ho-pa Yüeh's army. He and Chao Kuei had taken Yüeh's body back to P'ing-liang after his murder. Wu was an intrepid warrior and soon became a Great General. He entered the court when Hu took over its control and was made Duke of Cheng. His biography appears in CS 19.1a-6b and PS 65.1a-4a.

180. Among the other generals sent on the campaign was Wang Hsiung 王雄, an important member of the ruling group. He was killed in this campaign. See CS 19.23a-24a and PS 60.21b-22a.

181. The Ch'i forces appeared at Lo-yang on January 25, 565. Ta-hsi Wu and Yü-wen Hsien managed to prevent the whole army from fleeing, and when night fell, the troops were gathered at one place. Hsien wished to attack in the morning, but Ta-hsi Wu dissuaded him, and the army then withdrew. See CS 19.3b-4a. Hu is not mentioned in any of the accounts of this rout and probably had not gone past Hung-nung. See CS 5.9a and 12.2a.

182. Ling Prefecture was on the upper reaches of the Yellow River, near modern Ling-wu 靈武, in Ning-hsia.

183. The ancient site of Ch'ü-fu was a little east of the modern Tzu-yang 滋陽 in Shantung. This was the capital of Lu during the Ch'un-ch'iu period, and Confucius is said to have been born there. It was here that the Duke of Chou was enfeoffed by King Wu (Shih chi 33.1b; Chavannes, Mém. hist., IV, 89) and later by King Ch'eng (Couvreur, Li ki, I, 729). After the duke died, his son Po-ch'in 伯禽 received the fief (Shih chi 33.3a; Chavannes, Mém. hist., IV, 92-93).

184. After the well known discovery of the Duke of Chou's prayer in the coffer (Shu ching, Legge, III, 351-361), King Ch'eng, to honor the duke and at the same time to recompense him for his innocent sufferings, allowed the imperial suburban sacrifices to be performed in Lu. As Ssu-ma Ch'ien pointed out, Lu had this ritual and music of the Son of Heaven as a reward for the virtue of the Duke of Chou (Shih chi 33.7a; Chavannes, IV, 100). The Shih chi places the discovery after the death of the duke, and the honors were given to his son. The Shu, in the chapter referred to above, places the discovery during the lifetime of the duke.

185. The character 參, when used to denote the constellation,

-Notes to pp. 55-56-   -103-

has the pronunciation shen (see K'ang-hsi tzu-tien, s.v.); it was made up of the seven stars of Orion; see G. Schlegel, Uranographie chinoise, pp. 391 ff. The area of the state of Chin was associated with this constellation. See Tso chuan, Duke Chao, 1st year (Legge, V, 573, tr. p. 580a).

When King Ch'eng pacified this area, he gave it to his younger brother Yü 虞 as a fief. The amusing circumstances of this enfeoffment are told in the Shih chi, 39.1b (Chavannes, Mém. hist., IV, 251). The Tso chuan, Duke Chao, 15th year (Legge, V, 658, tr. p. 660a) mentions this enfeoffment in words closely resembling the present passage: i ch'u shen hsü 以處參虛, "in order to occupy the tract corresponding to the constellation Shen" (Legge's version modified in some details).

186. In the Tso chuan, Duke Hsi, 28th year (Legge, V, 200, tr. p. 202a), it is said that Ch'ung-erh as Duke of Chin used the great hunts (ta sou 大蒐) in order to demonstrate to his people the proper behavior. He believed that once they became trained in the chase their respectfulness would be more highly developed. The hunt was also used to train them to carry out orders without mistakes, train officers, etc.

These two men, the Duke of Chou on the one hand and Ch'ung-erh on the other, represent in this edict the two aspects of the Chou. The first was most influential with Heaven, while the power of the second was of a more terrestrial nature.

187. These words occur in the Tso chuan, Duke Hsiang, 19th year (Legge, V, 480, tr. p. 483a) and refer to that which should be recorded of a prince of a state.

188. On chü chen 居貞 see Chou-i 3.29a-b. T'i-tao 體道 occurs in the Chuang-tzu; see Nan-hua chen-ching 南華真經,

SPTK ed., 7.51b. The four characters appear in the same order as in our text in an epitaph written by Yü Hsin 庾信 for Tou-lu Ning 豆盧寧(d. 565); see Yü Tzu-shan chi 庾子山集, SPTK ed., 14.20a. Cf. the phrase chü-cheng t'i-tao 居正體道 in the Pien-ming lun 辯命論 of Liu Chün 劉峻 (462-520), Liu-ch'en-chu Wen-hsüan 六臣註文選, SPTK ed., 54.30b. Both expressions, separately and together, probably implied exalted character and position.

189. The right side was the position of honor; see Dai kanwa jiten 1851b, examples cited under yu 右, definition six.

190. Tung lung 棟隆 is the twenty-eighth hexagram of the I-ching (Chou i 3.31b). Legge translates (Yi king, p. 117), "The merit of the beam curving upward is that it does not bend toward what is below." K'ung Ying-ta says that it is able to lift up when in difficult straits (Chou i, loc. cit.).

191. Kuo pu 國步 appears in the Shih ching, Sang jou 桑柔 ode (Legge, IV, 520). Cf. also the Po-hua 白華 ode (ibid., p. 416) where the line t'ien pu chien-nan 天步艱難 occurs.

192. On tai shu 祚庶 see Chou i 8.14a with comments by the Chin scholar Han K'ang-po and K'ung Ying-ta. The language of Han K'ang-po's commentary on the passage immediately preceding may have been an influence (ibid., 8.13b).

On ju jen 如仁 see Analects 14.17 (Legge, I, 282) where Confucius twice says ju ch'i jen 如其仁 of Kuan Chung 管仲. Legge's interpolation of a relative pronoun is perhaps unwarranted. See various explanations of the phrase in Lun-yü cheng-i 論語正義 (Kuo-hsüeh chi-pen ts'ung-shu 國學基本叢書), p. 122.

193. The uniformity of the script and of the gauge of the wheels

-Notes to p. 56- -105-

of carts was in each case a symbol of political unification and order, associated especially with Ch'in Shih-huang-ti 秦始皇帝. See Shih chi 6.13b and Chavannes, Mém. hist., II, 135; discussed in D. Bodde, China's First Unifier (Leiden, 1938), pp. 147-161 and p. 179. See also the Chung-yung, Legge, I, 424.

194. Cf. pei wu tien-ts'e 備物典策 in the Tso chuan, 4th year of Duke Ting (Legge, V, 750, tr. p. 754a), where ts'e is probably rightly taken as "tablets" used for writing (although Legge's "historical records" for tien is perhaps questionable.)

195. Note the use of sheng 聲 and ming 明, first separately then together as here, in the Tso chuan, 2nd year of Duke Huan (Legge, V, 38, tr. p. 40a). The reference is to the acoustical and visual expressions of royal pomp, e.g., by means of bells and emblems of the celestial bodies.

196. Hsüan-hsüan chih yüeh 軒懸之樂 was an arrangement of musical instruments (probably bells, lithophones, etc.) suspended from bamboo frames and disposed on three sides, as contrasted with the four-sided scheme reserved for the emperor. In the case of the hsüan-hsüan arrangement, a privilege of the nobility (chu hou 諸侯), the southern side was lacking. See Chou li 23.9b-10b, comments of Cheng Hsüan 鄭玄 and Cheng Chung, 鄭衆, with additions by K'ung Ying-ta. The term ch'ü hsüan 曲縣/懸 also occurs, perhaps because of the curved shape (ibid.; see also K'ung-tzu chia-yü 孔子家語, SPTK ed., 9.27a, with comment of Wang Su 王肅). Cf. Ho Hsiu 何休 and Hsü Yen 徐彥 on hsüan ch'eng 軒城 (Kung-yang 公羊 26.11b-12a), where the same value is ascribed to hsüan.

The dancers in six rows (liu-i chih wu 六佾之舞) were reserved for the nobility (chu hou), and were second only to the eight rows of the sovereign; see the Tso chuan, 5th year of Duke Yin (Legge, V, 18, tr. p. 19b) and cf. Analects 3.1 (Legge, I, 154).

These two musical honors were associated together in grants of extraordinary power and privilege during the period Han to T'ang, in particular the awards of the so-called Nine Bestowals (chiu hsi 九錫). See San-kuo chih 三國志 1.36a for the award to Ts'ao Ts'ao 曹操, the first in which these musical gifts occur. (The passage, which is part of a citation composed for the occasion, was translated by von Zach from the text preserved in the Wen hsüan; see Die chinesische Anthologie [Cambridge, Mass., 1958], pp. 645-646.)

197. Yü-wen Chih, cognomen Tou-lo-t'u 豆羅突 (*törütü; see Boodberg, "The Language of the T'o-pa Wei," p. 171), was executed for attempted rebellion in 574. He was the sixth son of T'ai and a younger brother of the reigning emperor. The histories present him in a very unfavorable light. He was made Duke of Wei in 559 and Warden of Yung in 561. He was also Minister of Works at that time. When sent out on an expedition against Ch'en in 567 he suffered defeat. Because of this he was removed from office. Chih had pretended friendship toward Hu because of the latter's powerful position. He was now angered by his loss of office and asked the Emperor to intercede for him. The Emperor, who secretly desired to kill Hu, found in this wretched person an ally and plotted the affair with him. Chih's biography is found in CS 13.1b-3a and PS 58.1a-2a.

198. The Empress Dowager was the Lady Ch'ih-nu 叱奴, Mongol činoa, the secondary wife of Yü-wen T'ai. For her name see Bazin, p. 288 and Boodberg, "The Language of the T'o-pa Wei," pp. 177-178. She was from T'ai's native place of Tai

Commandery and was married to him after the establishment of the Western Wei. The annals of both the Chou shu and Pei shih place her elevation as Empress Dowager on July 3, 567 (CS 5.13a and PS 10.6a). However, her biographies in the two histories give 568 as the date (CS 9.3a and PS 14.13a). The Ch'ien-lung edition of the Chou shu gives the date in her biography as 566 (K'ai-ming ed., CS 9.2278a). The same discrepancy of a year occurs in the date of her death. The annals and Pei shih biography place it in 574 (CS 5.24a and PS 10.11b and 14.13a), while her biography in the Chou shu has 573 (CS 9.3a).

199. The "Admonishment on Wine" is the tenth book of the books of Shang in the Shu (Legge, III, 399-412). It is found in both the ku wen 古文 and chin wen 今文 texts. Until the Sung Dynasty, it was believed to be the words of the Duke of Chou. See Legge, III, 382, fn. The text warns of the harm excessive drinking works on a benevolent government.

200. Ho Ch'üan has no biography in the standard histories.

201. Wang Kuei (d. 578) was from T'ai-yüan in central Shansi. His father Kuang 光 had been noted for his martial bravery, and Kuei received an office through his influence. He became a close associate of the emperor Kao-tsu, but later, because of his opposition to the succession of the heir-apparent Yü-wen Yün 宇文贇, Kuei was killed at the latter's accession to the throne. His biography is in CS 40.3b-6b and PS 62.16a-18b.

202. Yü-wen Shen-chü (531-578) was a distant relative of the imperial family. His father Hsien-ho 顯和 was instrumental in persuading the Wei emperor to enter Shensi in 534. Shen-chü held some minor posts at the court, but after Hu's death rose to high office. He too was killed for his opposition to Yü-wen Yün's

accession. His biography is in CS 40. 7a-10b and PS 57. 18a-19b.

203. Yü-wen Hsiao-po (543-579), cognomen Hu-san 胡三, was a distant relative of the royal family. He was born on the same day as Kao-tsu and reared together with him. Like Wang Kuei and Yü-wen Shen-chü, Hsiao-po seems to have been a very forthright person. All three spoke out against the heir-apparent, and all three were killed by this madman. One gains the impression from the biographies of these three men that Kao-tsu was very successful in his choice of friends and companions. Hsiao-po's biography is in CS 40. 10b-14b and PS 57. 15b-18a.

204. Chang-sun Lan, cognomen Hsiu-yin 休因, was a T'o-pa from Honan. Kao-tsu had met him while serving in the provinces and, on ascending the throne, had made him a Great General. Lan's ming had been Shan 善, but Kao-tsu changed it to Lan, meaning "to inspect," since his duty was to inspect all papers before they were presented to the emperor. He also served the Sui for a short time. His biography is in Sui shu 51. 1a-2a and PS 22. 22b-23a.

205. Yü-wen Hui (see n. 29 above) was the second son of Hu and received the dukedom in 570.

206. Chih (see n. 70 above) was the third son of Hu. He received the dukedom as the result of being made the heir of Yü-wen P'u-t'i.

207. Ching was the fifth son of Hu. He received this dukedom after Chih, its previous holder, had been made Duke of Chü.

208. These were the sixth to eleventh sons of Hu. Hu also had at least one daughter, who married Su Wei 蘇威 (CS 23. 18a).

209. Hou-fu-hou Lung-en has been mentioned above; see n. 21. A prophecy of his end, as well as that of Hu, is described

in CS 47.17a-b.

210. Hou-fu-hou Wan-shou has no biography in the standard histories, but is mentioned in CS 29.22a.

211. Liu Yung has no biography in the standard histories.

212. Cheng Yüan-chieh has no biography in the standard histories. He was mentioned as the personal envoy sent by Hu to Wei Hsiao-k'uan at the time when the latter was negotiating with Ch'i about Hu's mother; see n. 93 above.

The Bureau of Internal and External [Affairs] (chung-wai fu 中外府) replaced the important department designated hsing-t'ai 行臺 in 553. This department had been headed by Yü-wen T'ai since the establishment of the Western Wei. See CS 33.15a; n.b. also CS 2.14a-b and 2.1a. Yü-wen Hu was evidently placed in charge of it in 561; see p. 36 above. The duties of the chung-wai-fu ssu-lu 中外府司錄 probably consisted chiefly in putting official documents in good literary form; see what is said of Li Ch'ang 李昶, who received this position in 559 (CS 38.13a-b).

213. On Li An see n. 77 above.

214. On tsao-li 皂隸 see Dai kanwa jiten 8203a-b (s.v. tsao) and 8204c-d (s.v. tsao-li). The term certainly designated a menial, in some cases specifically a stable-hand or groom. On the basis of the present text Wang Yi-t'ung concludes that Li An had been an enslaved cook; see "Slaves and other Comparable Social Groups during the Northern Dynasties (386-618)," HJAS, XVI (1953), 342. However, existing evidence does not seem to establish this assertion.

215. This passage is drawn from the Kung-yang chuan (9.9a and 22.2b). In both instances it is used to justify the murder of a rebellious member of the royal house. The Han commentator

Ho Hsiu 何休 explains that ch'in 親 refers to parents (ibid., 9.9a-b); however, "relatives" is more appropriate in the context. For early quotations and paraphrases of this passage see Ch'en Li 陳立 (1809-69), Kung-yang i-su 公羊義疏 (Shanghai, 1936), 26.662.

The passage was cited by Wang Mang 王莽 as the central idea of the Ch'un-ch'iu (Han shu 99C.3b; Dubs, Hist. of Former Han, III, 377). Yen Shih-ku, at this place, explains the sentence as "The Duke's son Ya 牙 was going to carry out murder and rebellion, so he was killed for it." Ya was the person concerned in the first use of the sentence in the Kung-yang chuan.

216. Sung wang 送往 is used in this same sense in the Tso chuan, Duke Hsi, 9th year (Legge, V, 153, tr. p. 154b).

217. This is Emperor Hsiao-min; see nn. 35 and 38 above. He was not awarded a posthumous name until after the death of Hu (CS 5.19b).

218. In the Tso chuan, 13th year of Duke Chao, a speaker states that the spirits were invited to choose the successor of King Kung 共王, who had no proper heir. This was done by burying a jade disc (pi 璧) in the court of the ancestral temple; one of the five favored sons by concubines was then considered elected by the spirits when he kowtowed "just over the jade disc" (tang pi 當璧); see Legge, V, 644, tr. p. 649b-650a.

219. Two characters have been deleted or lost from the text at this point, as noted in the text itself. This hiatus, present in other editions also, presumably dates from Sung times or earlier.

220. This sentence is taken from the "Prose-poem on the Western Capital" (Hsi ching fu 西京賦) of Chang Heng 張衡 (Liu-ch'en-chu Wen-hsüan 2.18b; tr. by von Zach, Die chine-

sische Anthologie, p. 9). The original, however, has sheng 生 for chia 加 as the first verb, and ch'eng 成 for sheng 生 as the second verb. Hsieh Tsung 薛綜, a third century commentator on this prose-poem, added that the down and feathers were meant to imply that these favored persons soared on high. The Shih chi (69.2a) has the sentence, "When the down and feathers are not yet complete, they cannot fly high."

221. "Three regions" (san fang 三方) refers to the threefold political division of China at this time, with Northern Chou and Northern Ch'i in the north and Ch'en in the south. Cf. use of the term for the Three Kingdoms by Lu Chi 陸機 (261-303) at the beginning of Pt. II of his Pien-wang lun 辨亡論 (Liu-ch'en-chu Wen-hsüan 53.33b).

222. Lofty roofs and carved walls were represented as a sure prelude to ruin; see Legge, III, 159. This chapter of the Shu (Wu-tzu chih ko 五子之歌) is probably not a genuine early work. Note that the same words occur in CS 31.14a, as a description of Yü-wen Hu's house.

223. This is drawn from Shih chi 4.22b and also appears in Liu-ch'en-chu Wen hsüan 44.9a.

224. King Ch'eng learned through divination that his dynasty was to last thirty generations, over seven hundred years; see Tso chuan, third year of Duke Hsüan (Legge, V, 292, tr. p. 293). In this text, the period of time would refer to the normal span of the dynasty, rather than a specific limit of time.

225. The two graphs for i 一 and tan 旦 are combined in the Po-na text of the Chou shu. This is evidently an inadvertence; hsüan 亘 makes poor sense. Other texts give i tan; e.g., the K'ai-ming edition of the Chou shu text, p. 2281b.

226. Chien-te, meaning "The Establishment of Virtue," lasted until the death of Kao-tsu in 578.

227. Yü-wen Hsün was the Duke of Chung-shan, his father's former fief. He was made Pillar of State in 571. For P'u Prefecture, see n. 26 above.

228. Yü-wen Sheng, cognomen Liu-chiu-t'u 六久突, the tenth son of T'ai, was made Duke of Yüeh in 559. He was active in some military ventures and acquitted himself with honor. He and his sons were killed by Yang Chien 楊堅 in 581 (CS 13.6a.)

229. On the type of carriage denoted sheng-chuan 乘傳 see comment of Ju Shun 如淳 translated by Dubs (Hist. of Former Han, I, 107, fn.). For a slightly different interpretation, see Tz'u hai, s.v.

230. On T'ung Prefecture see n. 84 above.

231. The name of Ch'ih-lo Hsieh (499-574) had originally been Yung 邕 ; it was changed because this was the tabooed name of Kao-tsu. Hsieh began his career in Chi Prefecture and passed successively into the hands of Ko Jung 葛榮, Erh-chu Chao 爾朱兆, and Kao Huan. He followed Tou T'ai's army into Shensi, and was again captured, this time by Yü-wen T'ai. Given some duties in T'ai's entourage, he proved his loyalty to his new master at the battle of Ho-ch'iao. He was sent to Shu where he was very successful in keeping the natives in submission. In 566 T'ai called him to court to report on the affairs of Shu and gave him the surname Yü-wen. He was recommended to Hu by some other men at the court and became Hu's right-hand man. He was rapidly promoted to Seneschal (chang shih 長史) and made a duke. At Hu's death he was removed from office, but he was restored to his noble rank in 574. He died in the same year.

His biography is in CS 11.17b-21a and PS 57.11a-12a.

The chang-shih were administrative heads of the staffs of civil and military leaders during this period.

Tai Commandery under the Northern Wei was located in northernmost Shansi, near the modern Ta-t'ung 大同 .

232. Feng Ch'ien (499-577), cognomen Yü-hua 羽化, began his career as an army officer under the Wei. He entered Shensi with the Emperor Hsiao-wu in 534 and displayed valor in the battles with Eastern Wei. When Hu took over the court, Ch'ien joined his staff and became a trusted officer. He was removed from office at Hu's death and died in 577 at his home. His biography is found in CS 11.21a-22b and PS 57.12a.

The biography (CS 11.17a) mentions Feng Ch'ien's appointment as "Chief Recorder of Hu's staff" (Hu fu ssu-lu 護府司錄). Probably this was the same office as Chief Recorder of the Interior and Exterior (see n. 212 above).

On Hung-nung see n. 17 above.

233. Yü-wen Shen was the fourth son of Hu. He does not have a biography in the standard histories and should not be confused with his distant kinsman of the same name whose biography appears in CS 27 and PS 57. His mission to the T'u-chüeh in the second month of 572 is mentioned in the annals (CS 5.18b; his name, however, is misprinted here, as noted by Liu Mau-tsai, Nachrichten, p. 506).

234. Yü-wen Te has no biography in the standard histories.

235. The Chou shu was written under the direction of Ling-hu Te-fen 令狐德棻 (583-666). The custom of putting brief comments at the end of each chapter dates from the Shih chi. These postfaces pointed the moral of the preceding chapter, since his-

tory was considered to have a didactic function.

The two biographies which follow that of Yü-wen Hu (<u>CS</u> 11. 17b-22b) have been omitted in the translation.

236. An elliptical quotation of <u>Analects</u> 9. 29 (Legge, I, 226). For the interpretation see comments of Chu Hsi 朱熹, <u>Ssu-shu chang-chü chi-chu</u> 四書章句集注 (Kuo-hsüeh chi-pen ts'ung-shu ed., Shanghai, 1935), <u>Lun-yü</u> 5. 67.

Chung-ni (lit., "Ni the second-born") was said to be the cognomen of Confucius. See <u>Shih chi</u> 47. 2a; Chavannes, <u>Mém. hist.</u>, V, 290-291, fn.; and n. 150 above.

237. I Yin was the advisor to T'ang 湯, the founder of the Shang dynasty. After T'ang's death, his grandson T'ai-chia succeeded him on the throne. The new king was supposedly an unrighteous youth. I Yin accordingly banished him to a palace at T'ung 桐 to reflect on his wrongdoings. The first <u>T'ai-chia</u> chapter of the <u>Shu ching</u> (a section of doubtful authenticity) tells of these events; see Legge, III, 199-203.

238. Tan was the given name (<u>ming</u> 名) of the Duke of Chou. This reference is to his regency on behalf of King Ch'eng. The epithet "Tender Youth" (<u>Ju tzu</u> 孺子) was applied to the young sovereign; see Legge, III, 357.

239. This is an allusion to Wang Mang, who was enfeoffed as Marquis of Hsin-tu 新都 by the Han (Dubs, <u>Hist. of Former Han</u>, III, 127.) He was regent for the last emperor of the Former Han and usurped the throne in A. D. 9 (ibid., pp. 255-259). For the removal of the tripods, see <u>Tso chuan</u>, Duke Hsüan, 3rd year (Legge, V, 292, tr. p. 293b).

240. The reference is to the overthrow of the Kingdom of Wei 魏 by the generals of the Ssu-ma 司馬 family in 265.

-Notes to pp. 62-63-   -115-

241. On wei chih 委質 and its graphic variants (委摯, 委贄) see Dai kanwa jiten 2945d-2946a. Ministers were sometimes likened to the arms and legs (ku kung 股肱) of the sovereign; see Legge, III, 79, 89 and 90.

242. Tsai heng 宰衡 was an honorific title given to Wang Mang. The explanation of its origin was that I Yin held the office of a-heng 阿衡 and the Duke of Chou that of t'ai-tsai 太宰 (Han shu 99A. 21b; Dubs, Hist. of Former Han, III, 185).

243. The Tso chuan, Duke Ai, 16th year (Legge, V, 844-845, tr. p. 847a) tells of a rebellious subject threatening with a sword a loyal person to get help in a nefarious project. The threat failed to move the man.

244. On the repentance of T'ai-chia in the palace at T'ung see n. 237 above.

The Wei-yang palace was built by Han Kao-tsu's minister Hsiao Ho 蕭何 in 200 B.C.; see Dubs, Hist. of Former Han, I, 118. The palace is described in the Ch'ang-an chih 長安志 of the eleventh-century scholar Sung Min-ch'iu 宋敏求 (Pi Yüan 畢沅 ed. in Ching-hsün-t'ang ts'ung-su 經訓堂叢書, blocks cut beginning 1783), 3.5a-9b. Before Han Wu-ti died in 87 B.C., he entrusted his young heir, the future Chao-ti, to the care of his faithful minister Ho Kuang 霍光 (Han shu 68.2a). The regent was very loyal to his charge and protected him from a plot instigated by the regent's own family. Although Chao-ti's life was brief, he appears to have died through natural causes in 74 B.C. in the Wei-yang Palace. See Dubs, II, 143-149 and 174.

These examples of the forbearance of ministers toward young or unworthy sovereigns are, of course, cited as a contrast to Yü-wen Hu's two acts of regicide; see pp. 14 and 15 above.

Bibliography

I. Chinese and Japanese Works

Ch'en Yin-k'o 陳寅恪. <u>Sui-T'ang chih-tu yüan-yüan lüeh-lun kao</u> 隋唐制度淵源略論稿. Academia Sinica, Institute of History and Philology. Monograph Series. Third printing, Shanghai, 1946.

Chou i 周易. In <u>Sung-pen Shih-san-ching chu-su fu chiao-k'an-chi</u> 宋本十三經注疏附校勘記, Juan Yüan 阮元 ed. Wood block ed., 1826.

Chou li 周禮. In <u>Shih-san-ching chu-su</u> (see <u>Chou i</u>).

Chou shu 周書. Compiled by Ling-hu Te-fen 令狐德棻 (583-666) and others. In <u>Po-na pen Erh-shih-ssu shih</u> 百衲本二十四史. Shanghai: Commercial Press, 1930-37. The text reproduced in the K'ai-ming edition of the <u>Twenty-five Histories</u> (Erh-shih-wu shih 二十五史, Shanghai: K'ai-ming shu-tien 開明書店, 1935) has occasionally been consulted.

Chou Yi-liang 周一良. <u>Lun Yü-wen Chou chih chung-tsu</u> 論宇文周之種族. Academia Sinica, Institute of History and Philology. Bulletin, VII (1939), 505-517.

Ch'un-ch'iu Tso chuan 春秋左傳. In <u>Shih-san-ching chu-su</u> (see <u>Chou i</u>).

Erh-ya 爾雅. In <u>Shih-san-ching chu-su</u> (see <u>Chou i</u>).

Han shu 漢書. Compiled by Pan Ku 班固 (A.D. 32-92) and others. In <u>Po-na pen Erh-shih-ssu shih</u> (see <u>Chou shu</u>).

Hou-Han shu 後漢書. Annals and biographies compiled by

Fan Yeh 范曄 (398-445); treatises compiled by Ssu-ma Piao 司馬彪 (ca. 265-305 or 306). In <u>Po-na pen Erh-shih-ssu shih</u> (see <u>Chou shu</u>).

Hsiao ching 孝經. In <u>Shih-san-ching chu-su</u> (see <u>Chou i</u>).

<u>Li chi</u> 禮記. In <u>Shih-san-ching chu-su</u> (see <u>Chou i</u>).

<u>Liu-ch'en-chu Wen-hsüan</u> 六臣注文選. Ed. and compiled by Hsiao T'ung 蕭統 (501-531). <u>Ssu-pu ts'ung-k'an</u> 四部叢刊 ed.

<u>Mao shih</u> 毛詩. In <u>Shih-san-ching chu-su</u> (see <u>Chou i</u>).

<u>Nan shih</u> 南史. Compiled by Li Yen-shou 李延壽 (fl. 629) and others. In <u>Po-na pen Erh-shih-ssu shih</u> (see <u>Chou shu</u>).

<u>Pei-Ch'i shu</u> 北齊書. Compiled by Li Te-lin 李德林 (531-591) and Li Po-yao 李百藥 (565-648). In <u>Po-na pen Erh-shih-ssu shih</u> (see <u>Chou shu</u>).

<u>Pei shih</u> 北史. Compiled by Li Yen-shou 李延壽 (fl. 629) and others. In <u>Po-na pen Erh-shih-ssu shih</u> (see <u>Chou shu</u>).

<u>Shang shu</u> 尚書. In <u>Shih-san-ching chu-su</u> (see <u>Chou i</u>).

<u>Shih chi</u> 史記. Compiled by Ssu-ma T'an 司馬談 (B.C. 180?-110) and Ssu-ma Ch'ien 司馬遷 (B.C. 145-86). In <u>Po-na pen Erh-shih-ssu shih</u> (see <u>Chou shu</u>).

Shiratori Kurakichi 白鳥庫吉, "Tōgo minzoku kō 東胡民族考," Pt. IV. <u>Shigaku zasshi</u> 史學雜誌, XXII (1911), 62-88.

<u>Sui shu</u> 隋書. Compiled by Wei Cheng 魏徵 (580-643) and others. In <u>Po-na pen Erh-shih-ssu shih</u> (see <u>Chou shu</u>).

<u>T'ung-tien</u> 通典. Compiled by Tu Yu 杜佑 (735-812). <u>Wan-yu wen-k'u</u> 萬有文庫 ed. Shanghai: Commercial Press, 1935.

<u>Tu-shih fang-yü chi-yao</u> 讀史方輿紀要. By Ku Tsu-yü

顧祖禹 (1631-1692 or 1693). T'ung-hua shu-wu 桐花書屋 ed., 1879.

Tzu-chih t'ung-chien 資治通鑑. By Ssu-ma Kuang 司馬光 (1019-1086). Ssu-pu ts'ung-k'an ed.

Tzu-chih t'ung-chien. By Ssu-ma Kuang, with commentary by Hu San-hsing 胡三省 (1230-1302). Punctuated typeset edition, 10 Western-style vols. Peking, 1956.

Wei shu 魏書. Compiled by Wei Shou 魏收 (506-572) and others. In Po-na pen Erh-shih-ssu shih (see Chou shu).

Yen-shih chia-hsün 顏氏家訓. By Yen Chih-t'ui 顏之推 (531-591+). In Pao-ching-t'ang ts'ung-shu 抱經堂叢書, photolithographic ed. Peking: Chih-li shu-chü 直隸書局, 1923.

II. Works in European Languages

Balazs, Etienne, "Le traité économique de 'Souei-Chou.'" TP, XLII (1953-54), 113-329.

Bazin, Louis, "Recherches sur les parlers T'o-pa (5e siècle après J.C.)." TP, XXXIX (1949-50), 228-329.

Boodberg, Peter A., "The Language of the T'o-pa Wei." HJAS, I (1936), 167-185.

Idem, "Marginalia to the Histories of the Northern Dynasties." HJAS, III (1938), 223-253; and IV (1939), 230-283.

Chavannes, Edouard. Documents sur les Tou-kioue (Turcs) occidentaux. Paris, n.d. Reprint of edition of Académie Impériale des Sciences de St. Petersbourg, 1900.

Idem. Les mémoires historiques de Se-ma Ts'ien. 5 vols. Paris, 1895-1905.

Couvreur, Seraphin. Li ki. Mémoires sur les bienséances et

les cérémonies. 2 vols. Paris, 1950.

Dubs, Homer H. The History of the Former Han Dynasty. 3 vols. Baltimore, 1932-55.

Eberhard, Wolfram. Das Toba-Reich Nordchinas. Leiden, 1949.

Franke, Otto. Geschichte des chinesischen Reiches. 5 vols. Berlin and Leipzig, 1930-52.

Goodrich, Chauncey S. Biography of Su Ch'o. University of California, Institute of East Asiatic Studies. Chinese Dynastic Histories Translations, No. 3. Berkeley and Los Angeles, 1953.

Karlgren, Bernhard. Grammata Serica. Script and Phonetics in Chinese and Sino-Japanese. Stockholm, 1940.

Legge, James. The Chinese Classics. 5 vols. in 8. Chinese reprint, 1939:
   I. Confucian Analects, The Great Learning, and the Doctrine of the Mean. Oxford, 1893.
   II. The Works of Mencius. Oxford, 1895.
   III. The Shoo King. London, n.d.
   IV. The She King. London, n.d.
   V. The Ch'un Ts'ew with the Tso Chuen. Hongkong, 1872.

Idem. The Yi King (Sacred Books of the East, XVI). Oxford, 1882.

Mather, Richard B. Biography of Lü Kuang. University of California, East Asia Studies. Chinese Dynastic Histories Translations, No. 7. Berkeley and Los Angeles, 1959.

Pelliot, Paul, "Neuf notes sur des questions d'Asie centrale." TP, XXVI (1929), 201-265.

des Rotours, Robert. Traité des fonctionnaires et Traité de l'armée traduits de la Nouvelle histoire des T'ang. 2 vols.

Leiden, 1947-48.

Wang Yi-t'ung, "Slaves and other Comparable Social Groups during the Northern Dynasties (386-618)." HJAS, XVI (1953), 293-364.

Wittfogel, Karl and Feng Chia-sheng. History of Chinese Society: Liao (907 to 1125). Transactions of the American Philosophical Society, New Series, XXXVI. Philadelphia, 1948.

von Zach, Erwin. Die chinesische Anthologie. Ubersetzungen aus dem Wen hsüan. Harvard-Yenching Institute Studies, XVIII. 2 vols. Cambridge, Mass., 1958.

Chinese Text

(<u>Chou</u> <u>shu</u> 11.1a–17b, 22b–23b)

列傳第三　　周書十一

晉蕩公護　令狐德棻　等撰
　　　　　叱羅協　馮遷

晉蕩公護字薩保太祖之兄邵惠公顥之少子也幼方正有志度特為德皇帝所愛異於諸兄年十一惠公薨隨諸父在葛榮軍中榮敗遷晉陽太祖之入關也護以年小不從普泰初自晉陽至平涼時年十七太祖諸子並幼遂委護以家務內外不嚴而肅太祖嘗歎曰此兒志度類我及出

臨夏州留護事賀拔岳岳之被害太祖至平涼以護爲都督從征侯莫陳悅破之後以迎魏帝功封水池縣伯邑五百戶大統初加通直散騎常侍征虜將軍以預定樂勳進爵爲公增邑通前一千戶從太祖擒竇泰復弘農破沙死戰河橋並有功遷鎮東將軍大都督八年進車騎大將軍儀同三司邙山之役護率衆先鋒爲敵人所圍都督侯伏侯龍恩挺身扞禦方得免是時趙貴等軍亦退太祖遂班師護坐免官尋復本位十二

年加驃騎大將軍開府儀同三司進封中山公增邑四百戶十五年出鎮河東遷大將軍與于謹征江陵護率輕騎為先鋒晝夜兼行乃遣神將攻梁臨邊鎮並拔之并擒其候騎進兵徑至江陵城下城中不意兵至惶窘失圖護又遣騎二千斷江津收舟艦以待大軍之至圍而克之以功封子會為江陵公初襄陽蠻帥向天保等萬有餘落恃險作梗及師還護率軍討平之初行六官拜小司空太祖西巡至牽屯山遇疾馳驛

召護,護至涇州見太祖而太祖疾已綿篤,謂護曰:吾形容若此,必是不濟,諸子幼小,寇賊未寧,天下之事屬之於汝,宜勉力以成吾志。護涕泣奉命,行至雲陽而太祖崩,護祕之,至長安乃發喪。時嗣子沖弱,彊寇在近,人情不安。護綱紀內外,撫循文武,於是眾心乃定。先是太祖常云:我得胡力。當時莫曉其旨,至是人以護字當之。尋拜柱國大祖。山陵畢,護以天命有歸,遣人諷魏帝,遂行禪代之事。孝閔帝踐祚,拜大司馬,封晉國公,邑一萬

戶趙貴獨孤信等謀襲護護因貴入朝追執之
黨與皆伏誅拜大冢宰時司會李植軍司馬孫
恒等在太祖之朝久居權要見護執政恐不見
容乃密要宮伯乙弗鳳張光洛賀拔提元進等
為腹心說帝曰護誅趙貴以來威權日盛謀臣
宿將爭往附之大小政事皆決於護以臣觀之將
不守臣節恐其滋蔓願早圖之帝然其言鳳等
又曰以先王之聖明猶委植恒以朝政今若左提右
挈何向不成且曹公常云我今夾輔陛下欲行周

公之事臣聞周公攝政七年然後復子明辟陛
下今日豈能七年若此乎深願不疑帝愈信之數
將武士於後園講習為執縛之勢護微知之乃
出植為梁州刺史恒為潼州刺史欲過其謀後
帝思植等每欲召之護諫曰天下至親不過兄
弟若兄弟自搆嫌隙他人何易可親太祖以陛
下富於春秋顧命託臣以後事臣既情兼家國
寔願竭其股肱若使陛下親覽萬機威加四海
臣死之日猶生之年但恐除臣之後姦回得逞其

欲非唯不利陛下亦恐社稷危亡臣所以勤勤懇
懇干觸天威者但不負太祖之顧託保安國家之
鼎祚耳不意陛下不照愚臣欵誠忽生疑阻且
臣既為天子兄復為國家宰輔知更何求而懷
異望伏願陛下有以明臣無惑讒人之口因泣涕久
之乃止帝猶猜之鳳等益懼密謀滋甚遂克日將
召羣公入醼執護誅之光洛具以其前後謀告護
護乃召柱國賀蘭祥小司馬尉遲綱等以鳳謀
告之祥等並勤護廢帝時抱領禁兵護乃遣

綱入宮召鳳等議事及出以次執送護第因罷散宿衛兵遣祥逼帝幽於舊邸於是召諸公卿畢集護流涕謂曰先王起自布衣躬親行陣勤勞王業三十餘年冠賊未平奄棄萬國寡人地則猶子親受顧命以略陽公既居正嫡與公等立而奉之革魏興周為四海主即位以來荒淫無度昵近羣小踈忌骨肉大臣重將咸欲誅夷若此謀遂行社稷必致傾覆寡人若死將何面目以見先王今日寧負略陽公不負社稷爾寧都公年德

兼茂仁孝聖慈四海歸心萬方注意今欲慶昏立明公等以為如何羣臣咸曰此公之家事敢不惟命是聽於是斬鳳等於門外并誅植恒等尋亦弑帝迎世宗於歧州而立之二年拜太師賜軺車冕服封子至為崇業郡公初改雍州刺史為牧以護為之并賜金石之樂武成元年護上表歸政帝許之軍國大事當委於護帝性聰睿有識量護深憚之有李安者本以鼎俎得寵於護稍被升擢位至膳部下大夫至是護乃密

令安因進食於帝加以毒藥帝遂寢疾而崩護立
高祖百官總已以聽於護自太祖為丞相左右
十二軍總屬相府太祖崩後皆受護處分凡所
徵發非護書不行護第七兵禁衞盛於宮闕
事無巨細皆先斷後聞保定元年以護為都督
中外諸軍事令五府總於天官或有希護旨云
周公德重魯立文王之廟以護功比周公宜用此
禮於是詔於同州晉國第立德皇帝別廟使護
祭焉三年詔曰大冢宰晉國公智周萬物道濟

天下所以克成我帝業安養我蒼生況親則懿昆任當元輔而同班羣品齊侯衆臣自今詔誥及百司文書並不得稱名以彰殊禮護抗表固讓初太祖創業即與突厥和親謀爲掎角共圖高氏是年乃遣柱國楊忠與突厥東伐破齊長城至幷州而還期後年更舉南北相應齊主大懼先是護母閻姬與皇第四姑及諸戚屬並沒在齊皆被幽縶護居宰相之後每遣閒使尋求莫知音息至是並許還朝且請和好四年

皇姑先至齊主以護既當權重乃留其母以為後圖仍令人為閽作書報護曰天地閉塞子母異所三十餘年存亡斷絕肝腸之痛不能自勝想汝悲思之懷復何可處吾自念十九入汝家今已八十矣既逢喪亂備嘗艱阻恒冀汝等長成得見一日安樂何期罪釁深重存沒分離吾凡生汝輩三男三女今日目下不覩一人興言及此悲纏肌骨賴皇齊恩邱差安衰暮又得汝楊氏姑及汝叔母紇于汝嫂劉新婦等同居頗亦自適

但為微有耳疾大語方聞行動飲食幸無多恙
今大齊聖德遠被特降鴻慈既許歸吾於汝
又聽先致音耗積稔長悲欻然獲展此乃仁俜
造化將何報德汝與吾別之時年尚幼小以前家
事或不委曲昔在武川鎮生汝兄弟大者屬鼠
次者屬兔汝身屬虵鮮于修禮起日吾之闔家
大小先在博陵郡住相將欲向左人城行至唐
河之北被定州官軍打敗汝祖及二叔時俱戰
亡汝叔母賀拔及兒元寶汝叔母紇干及兒菩

提并吾與汝六人同被擒捉入定州城未幾間將吾及汝送與元寶掌賀拔紇于各別分散寶掌見汝云我識其祖翁形狀相似時寶掌營在唐城内經停三日寶掌所掠得男夫婦女可六七十人悉送向京吾時與汝同被送限至定州城南夜宿同鄉人姬庫根家姑奴望見鮮于修禮營火語吾云我今走向本軍既至營遂告吾輩在此明旦日出汝叔將兵邀截吾及汝等還得向營汝時年十二共吾並乘馬隨軍可不記此事緣由也於後

吾共汝在受陽住時元寶菩提及汝姑兒賀蘭盛洛并汝身四人同學博士姓成為人嚴惡淩等四人謀欲加害吾汝共叔母等聞知各捉其兒打之唯盛洛無母獨不被打其後尒朱天柱亡歲賀拔阿斗泥在關西遣人迎家累時汝叔亦遣奴來富迎汝及盛洛等汝時著緋綾袍銀裝帶盛洛著紫織成績通身袍黃綾裏並乘騾同去盛洛小於汝等三人竝呼吾作阿摩敢如此之事當分明記之耳今又寄汝小時所著

錦袍表一領至宜撿看知吾舍悲戚多歷年祀
屬千載之運逢大齊之德矜老開恩許得相見
一聞此言死猶不朽況如今者勢必聚集禽獸
草木母子相依吾有何罪與汝分離念復何
福還望見汝言此悲喜死而更蘇世間所有
求此可得母子異國何處可求假汝貴極王公
富過山海有一老母八十之年飄然千里死亡
夕不得一朝蹔見不得一日同處寒不得汝衣饑不
得汝食汝雖窮榮極盛光耀世間汝何用為於吾

何益吾今日之前汝既不得申其供養事往何
論今日以後吾之殘命唯繫於汝爾戴天履地
中有鬼神勿云冥昧豈欺負汝楊氏姑今雖炎
暑猶能先發關河阻遠隔絕多年書依常體
慮汝致惑豈是以每存款賀兼亦載吾姓名當識
此理不以為怪護性至孝得書悲不自勝左右
莫能仰視報書曰䯀孑分崩遭遇災禍違離膝
下三十五年受形禀氣比曰知母子誰同薩保如此
不孝宿殃積戾唯應賜鐘豈悟網羅上嬰慈母

但立身行不貧一物明神有識宜見哀憐而子
爲公侯母爲俘隷熱不見母熱寒不見母寒衣
不知有無食不知饑飽泯如天地之外無由暫聞
晝夜悲號繼之以血分懷冤酷終此一生死若有
知望奉見於泉下爾不謂齊朝解網惠以德
音廲敦四姑並許於敖釈聞此皆魂爽飛越號
天叩地不能自勝四姑即蒙禮送平安入境以今
月十八日於河東拜見遙奉顏色崩動肝膈但
離絕多年存亡阻隔相見之始口未忍言唯叙

齊朝寬弘每存大德云與摩敦雖慶慰宮禁常蒙優禮今者來鄴恩遇彌隆矜哀聽許摩敦垂敕曲盡悲酷備述家事伏讀未周五情屠割書中所道無事敢忘摩敦年尊又加憂苦常謂寢膳毀損或多遺漏伏奉論述次第分明一則以悲一則以喜當鄉里破敗之日薩保年已十餘歲隣曲舊事猶目記憶況家門禍難親戚流離奉辭時節先後慈訓刻肌刻骨常纏心腑天長喪亂四海橫流太祖乘時齊朝撫運兩河三輔各值神

仁姑世母望絕生還彼朝以去夏之初德音爰發
已送仁姑許歸世母乃稱頻暑指尅來秋謂其
信必申要嘉言無奕今落木戒候冰霜行及方
為世母虛設詭詞未議言歸更徵酬答子女玉
帛既非所須保境寧民又云匪報詳觀此意全
乖本圖愛人以禮當吝為姑息要子責誠質親求
報實傷和氣有悖天經吾之周室太祖之天下
也焉可指國顧家殉名虧實不害所養斯旨仁
人卧鼓潛鋒孰非深計若令迭爭尺寸兩競錐

期今日得通家問伏紙嗚咽言不宣忝蒙寄薩
保別時所留錦袍表年歲雖久宛然猶識抱此
悲泣至于拜見事歸忍死知復何心齊朝不即
發遣更令與護書要護重報往返再三而竟
不至朝議以其失信令有司穢齊日夫有義則
存無信不立山岳猶輕兵食非重故言指言弗違
重耳所以尊國祝史無媿隨會所以為盟未有
司牧生民君臨有國可以忘義而多食言者也
自數屬屯夷時鐘圮隔皇家親戚淪陷三紀

機原其事跡非相負背太祖升遐未定天保
保屬當猶子之長親受顧命雖身居重任職當
憂責至於歲時稱慶子孫在庭顧視悲摧心情
繼絕胡顏履戴負媿神明霈然之恩既以霑洽
愛敬之至施及傍人草木有心禽魚感澤況在
人倫而不銘戴有家有國信義為本伏產永期
已應有日一得奉見慈顏畢生願生死肉骨
豈過今恩負山戴岳未足勝荷二國分隅理無
書信主上以彼朝不絕子母之恩亦賜許奉答不

刀瓦震長平則趙分為二兵出函谷則韓裂衣為三安得猶全謂無損益大家宰位隆將相情兼家國銜悲茹血分畢究魂豈意嗟指可尋倚門應至徒聞善始卒無令終百辟震驚三軍憤悗不為孝子當作忠臣去歲北軍深入數俘城下雖曰班師餘功未遂今茲馬首南向更期重入晉人角之我之職矣聞諸道路早已戒嚴非直北拒又將南略儻欲自送此之願也如或嬰城未能求敵詰朝請見與石周旋為惠不終祗增深怨愛

親無慢垂訓尼父矜鄒竇老貽則周文環球之
義事不由此自應內省豈宜有閒於書未送而
母至舉朝慶悅大赦天下護與毋聯歡多年一
旦聚集凡所資奉窮則極華盛四時伏臘高
祖率諸親戚行家人之禮稱觴上壽榮貴之極
振古未聞是年也突厥復率衆赴期護以齊
氏初送國親未欲即事征討復慮失信蕃夷更
生邊患不得已遂請東征九月詔曰神若軒皇
尚云三戰聖如姬武且曰戎狐矢之威干戈之用

帝王大器誰能去兵太祖丕受天明造我周室日月所照罔不率從高氏乘釁跋扈竊有冀世濟其惡腥穢彰聞皇天震怒假手突厥驅略汾晉掃地無遺季孟勢窮伯珪日蹙坐待滅亡鑒之愚智故突厥班師仍屯彼境更集諸部傾國齊至星流電擊數道俱進期在仲冬同會于鄴大冢宰晉公朕之懿昆任隆伊呂平一宇宙惟公是屬朕當親執斧鉞廟廷祗受有司宜勒衆軍量程赴集進止遲速委公處

分於是徵二十四軍及左右廂散隸及秦隴巴蜀之兵諸蕃國之衆二十萬人十月帝於廟庭授護斧鉞出軍至潼關乃遣柱國尉遲迥率精兵十萬爲前鋒大將軍權景宣率山南之兵出豫州少師楊檦出軹關護連營漸進屯軍弘農迴攻圍洛陽柱國公憲鄭國公達奚武等營於邙山護性無戎略且此行也又非其本心故師出雖久無所克獲護本令漸斷河陽之路過其救兵然後同攻洛陽使其內外隔絕諸將以

為齊兵必不敢出唯斥候而已窘連日陰霧齊騎直前圍洛之軍一時潰散唯尉遲迥率數十騎扞敵齊公憲又督邙山諸將拒之乃得全軍而返權景宣攻克豫州尋以洛陽圍解亦引軍退楊檦於軹關戰没護於是班師以無功與諸將稽首請罪帝弗之責也天和二年護母薨尋有詔起令視事四年護巡歷北邊城鎮至靈州而還五年又詔曰光宅曲阜魯用郊天之樂地處象墟晉有大蒐之禮所以言時計功昭德

紀行使持節太師都督中外諸軍事柱國大將軍大家宰晉國公體道居貞含和誕德地居戚右才表棟隆國步艱難寄深夷險皇綱締構事均休戚故以迹冥殆庶理契如仁今文軌尚隔方隅猶阻典策未備聲明多闕宜賜軒懸之樂六佾之舞護性甚寬和然暗於大體自恃建立之功久當權軸凡所委任皆非其人兼諸子貪殘僚屬縱逸恃護威勢莫不肆政害民上下相蒙曾無疑慮高祖以其暴慢密與衛王直圖之七

年三月十八日護自同州還帝御文安殿見護訖引護入含仁殿朝皇太后先是帝於禁中見護常行家人之禮護謁太后太后必賜之坐帝立侍焉至是護將入帝謂之曰太后春秋既尊頗好飲酒不親朝謁或廢引進喜怒之間時有乖爽比雖犯顏屢諫未蒙垂納兄今既朝拜願更啟請因出懷中酒誥以授護曰以此諫太后護既如帝所戒讀示太后未訖帝以玉珽自後擊之護踣於地又令宦者何泉以御刀斫之泉惶懼斫

不能傷時衛王直先匿於戶內乃出斬之初帝欲圖護王軌宇文神舉宇文孝伯頗豫其謀是日軌等並在外更無知者殺護訖乃召宮伯長孫覽等告之即令收護子柱國譚國公會大將軍莒國公至崇業公靜正平公軌嘉及軌基軌光軌尉軌祖軌威等并柱國侯伏侯龍恩龍恩弟大將軍萬壽大將軍劉勇中外府司錄尹公正袤傑膳部下大夫李安等於殿中殺之齊王憲曰帝曰李安出自皂隸所典唯庖廚而已既不預時政

未足加戮高祖曰公不知耳世宗之崩安所爲也
十九日詔曰君親無將將而必誅太師大家寧晉
公護地寔宗親義兼家國爰初草創同濟艱難
遂任摠朝權寄深國命不能竭其誠効罄以
力盡事君之節申送往之情朕兄故略陽公英
風秀遠神機頴悟地居聖偭禮歸當璧遺訓
在耳忍害先加永尋推割貫切骨髓世宗明皇
帝聰明神武欽二字藏智護內懷凶悖外託尊崇
凡厥臣民誰不怨憤朕纂承洪基十有三載委

政師輔責成宰司護志在無君義違臣節懷
茲蕫珪每逞彼狼心任情暴肆行威福朋黨
相扇貽悞公行所好加羽毛所惡生瘡痏朕
已菲躬情存庶政每思施寬惠下輒抑而不行
遂使戶凋殘征賦勞劇家無日給民不聊生且
三方未定邊隅尚阻疆場待戎旗之備武夫資
扞城之力侯伏龍恩萬壽劉勇等未効庸勳
先居上將高門峻宇甲第周牆寔繁有徒同惡
相濟民不見德唯利是眂百姓嗷數道路以目

舍生業業相顧鉗口常恐七百之基忽焉顛墜億兆之命旦陷危亡累祖宗之靈下負蒼生之責今肅正典刑護已即罪其餘凶黨咸亦伏誅氛霧既清遐邇同慶朝政惟新兆民更始可大赦天下改天和七年爲建德元年護世子訓爲蒲州刺史其夜遣柱國越國公盛乘傳往蒲州徵訓赴京師至同州賜死護長史代郡叱羅協司錄弘農馮遷及所親任者皆除名護子昌城公深使突厥遣開府宇文德齎璽書就殺之

史臣曰仲尼有言可與適道未可與權夫道者率禮之謂也權者反經之謂也苟非禮由乎正理易以

三年詔復護及諸子先封謚護曰蕩並改葬之

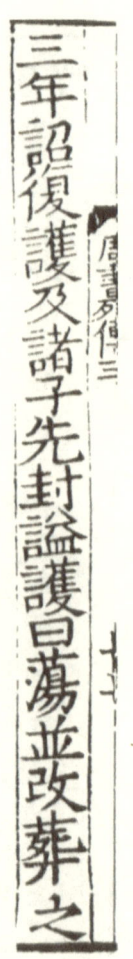

成佐世之功反經繫乎非常難以定匡時之業
故得其人則治伊尹放太甲周旦相孺子是也
不得其人則亂新都遷漢鼎晉氏傾魏族是也
是以先王明上下之序聖人重君臣之分委質
同於股肱受爵均其休戚當其親受顧託位居
宰衡雖復承利劒臨沸鼎不足以譽其慮據帝
圖君海內不足以回其心若斯人者固以功與
山嶽爭其高名與穹壤齊其父矣有周受命之
始宇文護定預艱難及太祖崩俎諸子冲幼羣

公懷等夷之志天下有去就之心卒能變魏為周俾危獲乂者護之力也向使加之以禮讓繼之以忠貞桐宮有悔過之期未央終天年之數則前史所載焉足以道哉然護寡於學術昵近羣小威福在已征伐自出有人臣無君之心為人主不堪之事忠孝大節也違之而不疑廢弒至逆也行之而無悔終於身首橫分妻孥為戮不亦宜乎

列傳第三

周書十一

Index

a-ma-tun (ma-tun), 43, 46, 47, 88 n. 112, 89 n. 120.

army, organization of, 10, 39.

Army Constable, 34.

Assistant Constable, 36, 75 n. 54, 76 n. 55.

Assistant Minister of Public Works, 32.

Cavalier Attendant with Direct Access, 31, 66 n. 14.

Chang Kuang-lo, 28 n. 38, 34, 36, 73 n. 47, 74 n. 50.

chang-shih: see Seneschal.

Chang-sun Chien, 72 n. 42.

Chang-sun Lan, 58, 108 n. 204.

Chang-sun Seng-yen, 72 n. 42.

Ch'ang-an, 16, 33, 70 n. 34, 78 n. 67, n. 71, 80 n. 84, 89 n. 123.

Ch'ang-li, 3, 26 n. 6.

Ch'ang-p'ing, 50, 93 n. 142.

Chao (state), 50.

Chao Kuei, 8, 9, 10, 11, 13, 20, 31, 34, 67 n. 22, 71 n. 40, 75 n. 54, 101 n. 179.

ch'e-chi ta-chiang-chün i-t'ung san-ssu: see Great General of Chariots and Cavalry with Dignities Equal to those of the Three Ministers.

chen-tung chiang-chün: see General who Garrisons the East.

Ch'en (state), 17, 106 n. 197.

cheng-lu chiang-chün: see General who Campaigns against the Caitiff.

Cheng Yüan-chieh (Duke of Yin), 58, 109 n. 212.

Ch'eng, King, 18, 20, 102 n. 183, n. 184, 103 n. 185, 111 n. 224.

Chi K'u-ken, 42, 86 n. 103.

Chi Prefecture, 53.

Ch'i, Duke of: see Yü-wen Hsien.

Ch'i, Prince of: see Yü-wen Hsien.

Ch'i Prefecture, 38, 78 n. 67.

Chiang-ling, 9, 32, 68 n. 27, 69 n. 30, 100 n. 175.

Chief Minister, 39.

Chief Recorder, 61.

Chief Recorder of the Interior and Exterior, 58, 109 n. 212.

Ch'ien-t'un Mountain, 33, 70 n. 32.

Chih Pass, 16, 54, 55, 101 n. 177.

Ch'ih-lieh-fu Kuei, 85 n. 96.

Ch'ih-lo Hsieh, 61, 112 n. 231.

Ch'ih-nu, Lady (Empress Dowager), 57, 106 n. 198.

Ch'ih-nu Hsing, 72 n. 42.

Chin (family of), 62.

Chin (state), 51, 55.

Chin, Duke of (Yü-wen Hu), 34, 39, 56, 59.

Chin River, 53.

Chin-yang, 30, 65 n. 7, 87 n. 105, n. 106, 99 n. 167.

Ch'in, 54, 100 n. 171.

Ch'in River, 5, 26 n. 17.

Ching Prefecture, 33, 70 n. 33.

Ching K'o, 88 n. 115.

Chou, Duke of (Tan), 18, 19, 20, 21, 22, 23, 34, 39, 62, 74 n. 49, 76 n. 57, 102 n. 183, n. 184, 103 n. 186, 107 n. 199, 114 n. 238, 115 n. 242.

chu-kuo: see Pillar of State.

chu-kuo ta-chiang-chün: see Pillar of State Great General.

Ch'ü-fu, 55, 102 n. 183.

Ch'üan Ching-hsüan, 16, 54, 55, 100 n. 174.

chün ssu-ma: see Army Constable.

Chung-ni: see Confucius.

Chung-shan, 32, 67 n. 25.

chung-wai-fu ssu-lu: see Chief Recorder of the Interior and Exterior.

Ch'ung-erh, 49, 90 n. 130, 92 n. 137, 94 n. 148, 103 n. 186.

Confucius (Chung-ni; Father Ni), 51, 94 n. 150, 102 n. 183, 104 n. 192, 114 n. 236.

ebüsün, 24 n. 2.

Empress Dowager: see Ch'ih-nu, Lady.

emüne, 24 n. 2.

Erh-chu Jung, 4, 5, 9, 72 n. 41, 73 n. 46, 87 n. 108.

Erh-chu T'ien-kuang, 5, 6, 9, 70 n. 32.

Father Ni: see Confucius.

Fen River, 53, 98 n. 163.

Feng Ch'ien, 61, 113 n. 232.

General Accountant, 34, 72 n. 44.

General who Campaigns against the Caitiff, 31, 66 n. 15.

General who Garrisons the East, 31.

Governor-director, 30, 31, 65 n. 11.

Governor-director of Internal and External Military Affairs, 39, 56.

Grand Tutor, 38, 56, 59, 70 n. 35.

Great Chancellor, 10, 34, 51, 56, 59, 74 n. 35.

Great Constable, 33, 71 n. 39, 75 n. 54.

Great General, 54, 56, 58, 71 n. 39, 72 n. 44, 74 n. 50.

Great General of Cavalry, 31, 67 n. 23.

Great General of Chariots and Cavalry with Dignities Equal to those of the Three Ministers, 31, 67 n. 19.

Great Governor-director, 31, 67 n. 18.

Han (state), 50, 62.

Han River, 9.

-Index-

Han-ku Pass, 50, 93 n. 143.

Ho Ch'üan, 58, 107 n. 200.

Ho-ch'iao, 7, 31, 66 n. 17, 112 n. 231.

Ho-kan, née, 41, 42, 85 n. 98, n. 100.

Ho-lan Hsiang (Ho-lan Sheng-lo), 14, 36, 43, 75 n. 54, 87 n. 106.

Ho-lan Sheng-lo: see Ho-lan Hsiang.

Ho-pa, née, 42, 85 n. 100.

Ho-pa A-tou-ni: see Ho-pa Yüeh.

Ho-pa Sheng, 9, 72 n. 41.

Ho-pa T'i, 34, 73 n. 47.

Ho-pa Yüeh (Ho-pa A-tou-ni), 5, 6, 9, 30, 43, 65 n. 10, 72 n. 41, 87 n. 109, 101 n. 179.

Ho-tung, 32, 46, 68 n. 26.

Hou-fu-hou Lung-en, 31, 58, 60, 67 n. 21, 108 n. 209.

Hou-fu-hou Wan-shou, 58, 60, 109 n. 210.

Hou-mo-ch'en Ch'ung, 9, 11, 14, 21, 71 n. 40.

Hou-mo-ch'en Yüeh, 6, 30, 65 n. 12, 70 n. 32.

Hsia Prefecture, 30, 65 n. 9, 78 n. 67.

Hsiang T'ien-pao, 32, 69 n. 30.

Hsiang-yang, 32, 69 n. 30.

Hsiao Ch'a, 8, 9.

Hsiao I, 8, 9.

Hsiao-min, Emperor: see Yü-wen Chüeh.

hsiao ssu-k'ung: see Assistant Minister of Public Works.

hsiao ssu-ma: see Assistant Constable.

Hsien, Prince: see Yü-wen Hsien.

Hsien-pei, 24 n. 3.

Hsien-yü Hsiu-li, 4, 42, 43, 67 n. 25.

Hsin-tu, 62.

Hsiu-jung, 4.

Hsiung-nu, 24 n. 3.

Hsüan-t'u, 3, 26 n. 7.

Hsüeh Shan, 28 n. 38.

Hung-nung, 7, 16, 17, 31, 54, 61, 66 n. 17, 102 n. 181.

I Yin, 62, 99 n. 168, 114 n. 237, 115 n. 242.

I-fu Feng, 34, 37, 38, 73 n. 46.

I-tou-kuei, 3.

Imperial Commissioner Holding the Seal of Command, 55.

Ju-ju: see Juan-juan.

Juan-juan (Ju-ju), 4, 28 n. 39, 43, 82 n. 90, 86 n. 104.

k'ai-fu: see Palatine.

k'ai-fu i-t'ung san-ssu: see Palatine with Dignities Equal to those of the Three Ministers.

Kao Huan, 6, 7, 8, 78 n. 70, 82 n. 90, 83 n. 92, 112 n. 231.

Kao-tsu: see Yü-wen Yung.

Ko Jung, 4, 5, 9, 30, 72 n. 41, 112 n. 231.

kung-po: see Major-domo.

Lai Fu, 43.

Li An, 38, 58, 79 n. 77, 109 n. 213.

Li Chih, 34, 35, 72 n. 44, 78 n. 66.

Li Hu, 10.

Li Pi, 9, 10, 13, 14, 71 n. 40.

Li Yüan, 9, 72 n. 44, 78 n. 66.

Liang (state), 8, 69 n. 30.

Liang Prefecture, 35, 74 n. 51.

Ling Prefecture, 55, 102 n. 182.

Liu, née, 41.

Liu Yung, 58, 60, 109 n. 211.

Lo-yang, 3, 6, 7, 8, 16, 54, 55, 66 n. 17, 67 n. 20, 102 n. 181.

Lower Grandee of the Imperial Kitchen, 38, 58, 79 n. 78.

Lu (state), 39, 55, 102 n. 183.

Lung, 54, 100 n. 171.

Lüeh-yang, Duke of: see Yü-wen Chüeh.

ma-tun: see a-ma-tun.

Major-domo, 34, 73 n. 46.

Man tribes, 15, 32, 69 n. 30.

Mang Hills, 8, 16, 31, 54, 55, 67 n. 20.

Minor Tutor, 54.

Mo-ch'i Chi-t'ung, 72 n. 42.

mu: see Warden.

Mu-han Qaghan, 28 n. 39, 83 n. 91.

Mu-jung (clan), 3.

Mu-jung Huang (Yüan-chen), 3, 25 n. 6.

Mu-jung Yüan-chen: see Mu-jung Huang.

Ning-tu, Duke of: see Yü-wen Yü.

Office of Heaven, 39, 80 n. 83.

Pa, 54, 100 n. 171.

Palatine, 61, 67 n. 24, 72 n. 42.

Palatine with Dignities Equal to those of the Three Ministers, 32.

p'iao-chi ta-chiang-chün: see Greatt General of Cavalry.

Pillar of Heaven, 43.

Pillar of State, 33, 36, 40, 54, 56, 58, 61, 71 n. 37, 72 n. 44, 76 n. 55, 112 n. 227.

Ping Prefecture, 40, 53, 83 n. 91.

P'ing-liang, 30, 65 n. 8, 101 n. 179.

Po-ling Commandery, 42, 85 n. 99.

P'o-liu-han Pa-ling, 3, 72 n. 41.

Prefect, 35, 61, 75 n. 51.

P'u Prefecture, 61.

-Index-

Sa-pao, 30, 45, 47, 48, 64 n. 1, 71 n. 36.

Seneschal, 61, 112 n. 231.

Sha-yüan, 7, 31, 66 n. 17.

Shan-nan, 54, 100 n. 175.

shan-pu hsiao-ta-fu: see Lower Grandee of the Imperial Kitchen.

shao-shih: see Minor-tutor.

Shih-tsung: see Yü-wen Yü.

Shou-yang, 43, 87 n. 105.

Shu, 54, 100 n. 171, 112 n. 231.

Shui-ch'ih District, 31, 65 n. 13.

ssu-hui: see General Accountant.

ssu-lu: see Chief Recorder.

Sui Hui, 49, 90 n. 131.

Sun Heng, 34, 35, 73 n. 45.

ta chung-tsai: see Great Chancellor.

Ta-hsi Wu, 14, 16, 54, 83 n. 91, 101 n. 179, 102 n. 181.

ta ssu-k'ou: see Minister of Crime.

ta ssu-k'ung: see Minister of Public Works.

ta ssu-ma: see Great Constable.

ta ssu-t'u: see Minister of Education.

ta tsung-po: see Minister of Rites.

ta tu-tu: see Great Governor-director.

Tai Commandery, 61, 68 n. 25, 106 n. 198, 113 n. 231.

T'ai-hang Mountains, 16.

t'ai-shih: see Grand Tutor.

T'ai-tsu: see Yü-wen T'ai.

Tan of Chou: see Chou, Duke of.

Tan-yang, 9.

T'an, Duke of: see Yü-wen Hui.

T'ang City, 42, 86 n. 102.

T'ang River, 42, 85 n. 99.

Te-huang, Emperor: see Yü-wen Hung.

t'ien-chu: see Pillar of Heaven.

Ting Prefecture, 42.

T'o-pa Huang, 26 n. 6.

Tou T'ai, 7, 31, 66 n. 16, 112 n. 231.

Tou-lu Ning, 14, 69 n. 30.

Tso-jen City, 42, 85 n. 99.

Tu Lo-chou, 4, 5.

Tu-ku Hsin, 7, 9, 10, 11, 13, 20, 34, 71 n. 40, 72 n. 41, n. 42.

tu-tu: see Governor-director.

T'u-chüeh, 15, 16, 17, 28 n. 39, 40, 52, 53, 61, 83 n. 91, 84 n. 93, 96 n. 155, 113 n. 233.

T'u-men Qaghan, 28 n. 39.

T'u-yü-hun, 15.

Tuan Shao, 95 n. 153.

t'ung-chih san-chi ch'ang-shih: see Cavalier Attendant with Direct Access.

T'ung Palace, 63.

T'ung Pass, 6, 7, 8, 16, 54, 88 n. 110.

T'ung Prefecture (Shensi), 39, 57, 61, 80 n. 84, 112 n. 230.

T'ung Prefecture (Szechwan), 35, 74 n. 51.

tz'u-shih: see Prefect.

Wang Hsiung, 101 n. 180.

Wang Kuei, 58, 107 n. 201, 108 n. 203.

Wang Lung-jen, 72 n. 42.

Warden, 38, 78 n. 71, 106 n. 197.

Wei (clan), 62.

Wei, Prince of: see Yü-wen Chih.

Wei Hsiao-k'uan, 9, 84 n. 93, 109 n. 212.

Wei K'o-ku (Wei K'o-kuei), 3, 26 n. 9.

Wei K'o-kuei: see Wei K'o-ku.

wen-an tien: see Hall of Civil Tranquillity.

Wen, King, 39, 52, 95 n. 151.

Wo-yeh Garrison, 3.

Wu, King, 18, 22, 96 n. 157, 102 n. 183.

Wu-ch'uan Garrison, 3, 9, 10, 26 n. 7, 42, 65 n. 10, 68 n. 25, 72 n. 41.

Yang, Aunt, 41, 45, 85 n. 97, 91 n. 135.

Yang Chung, 9, 10, 14, 16, 40, 82 n. 89, 83 n. 91.

Yang Piao, 16, 54, 55, 101 n. 176.

Yeh, 16, 46, 53, 99 n. 167.

Yen, Madam, 40, 52, 55, 92 n. 135.

Yin, Duke of: see Cheng Yüan-chieh.

Yü Chin, 8-9, 11, 12, 32, 68 n. 27, 71 n. 40.

Yü Prefecture, 54, 55, 100 n. 174.

Yü-ch'ih Chiung, 16, 54, 55, 78 n. 69, 100 n. 173.

Yü-ch'ih Kang, 14, 36, 76 n. 55, 100 n. 173.

Yü-wen (clan), 2, 24 n. 3-4.

Yü-wen Ch'ien-chi, 58.

Yü-wen Ch'ien-chia, 58.

Yü-wen Ch'ien-kuang, 58.

Yü-wen Ch'ien-tsu, 58.

Yü-wen Ch'ien-wei, 58.

Yü-wen Ch'ien-wei, 58.

Yü-wen Chih (Duke of T'an; third son of Yü-wen Hu), 38, 58, 78 n. 70, 108 n. 206.

Yü-wen Chih (Prince of Wei; son of Yü-wen T'ai), 57, 58, 106 n. 197.

Yü-wen Ching, 38, 58, 108 n. 207.

-Index-

Yü-wen Chou, 68 n. 29, 85 n. 98.

Yü-wen Chüeh (Duke of Lüeh-yang; Emperor Hsiao-min), 12, 13, 33, 37, 59, 70 n. 35, 71 n. 38, 76 n. 58, 78 n. 66, n. 67, 110 n. 217.

Yü-wen Hao, 3, 30, 64 n. 2, 68 n. 29.

Yü-wen Hsiao-po, 58, 108 n. 203.

Yü-wen Hsien (Duke of Ch'i; Prince of Ch'i; Duke Hsien; Prince Hsien), 16, 21, 54, 55, 58, 101 n. 178, 102 n. 181.

Yü-wen Hsün, 61, 112 n. 227.

Yü-wen Hui (Duke of T'an), 32, 58, 68 n. 29, 108 n. 205.

Yü-wen Hung (Te-huang Emperor), 3, 30, 39, 64 n. 5.

Yü-wen Kuang-pao (Yü-wen Yüan-pao), 42, 43, 83 n. 92, 85 n. 100.

Yü-wen Kuei, 28 n. 38.

Yu-wen Lien, 4, 65 n. 10, 85 n. 100.

Yü-wen Ling, 3.

Yü-wen Lo-sheng, 4, 5, 78 n. 70, 85 n. 98.

Yü-wen P'u-t'i, 42, 43, 78 n. 70, 83 n. 92, 85 n. 100.

Yü-wen Shen, 61, 113 n. 233.

Yü-wen Shen-chü, 58, 107 n. 202, 108 n. 203.

Yü-wen Sheng, 28 n. 38.

Yü-wen Sheng (son of Yü-wen T'ai), 61, 112 n. 228.

Yü-wen Shih-fei, 3, 83 n. 92, 84 n. 96.

Yü-wen T'ai (T'ai-tsu), 4-13 passim, 17, 21, 22, 29 n. 39, 30, 31, 32, 33, 39, 47, 50, 52, 59, 63, 64 n. 3, 65 n. 9, n. 10, 70 n. 34, 72 n. 41, 75 n. 54, 76 n. 55, 77 n. 62, 78 n. 67, 85 n. 98, 92 n. 139, 106 n. 197, n. 198, 112 n. 231.

Yü-wen Tao, 3, 27 n. 35, 70 n. 32, 84 n. 96.

Yü-wen Te, 61, 113 n. 234.

Yü-wen Yü (Duke of Ning-tu; Shih-tsung), 37, 38, 58, 59, 77 n. 62, 78 n. 67, 80 n. 79.

Yü-wen Yüan-pao: see Yü-wen Kuang-pao.

Yü-wen Yung (Kao-tsu), 29 n. 39, 38, 57, 58, 80 n. 79, n. 80.

Yüan Chin, 34, 73 n. 47.

Yüan Hsin, 10.

Yüan Li (Yüan Pao-chang), 42, 85 n. 100, 86 n. 101.

Yüan Pao-chang: see Yüan Li.

Yün-yang, 33, 70 n. 34.

Yung Prefecture, 38, 79 n. 71, 106 n. 197.

GENEALOGICAL CHA

(On the paternal side, only those na

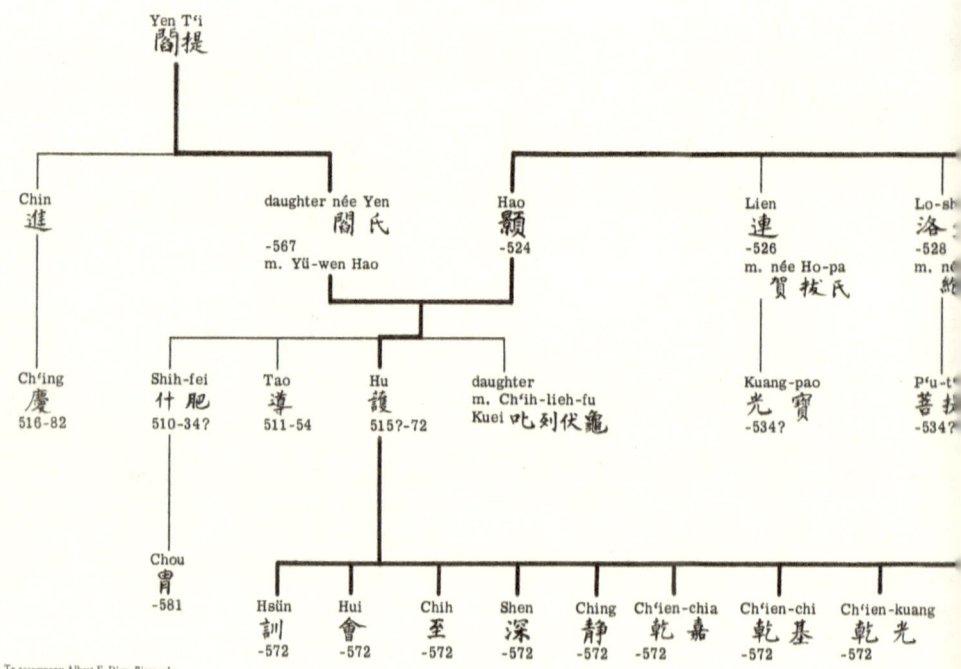

To accompany Albert E. Dien, *Biography of Yü-Wen Hu*, Chinese Dynastic Histories Translations, No. 9.

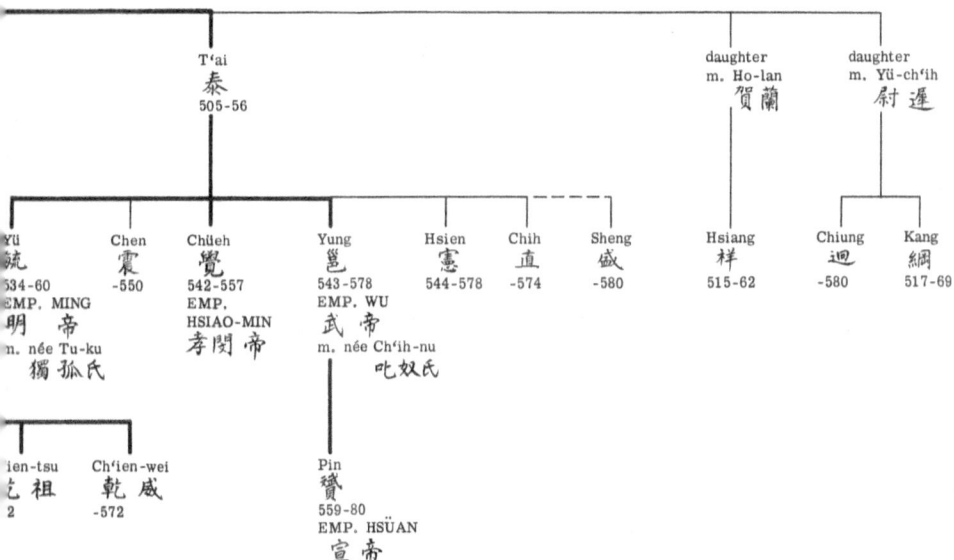

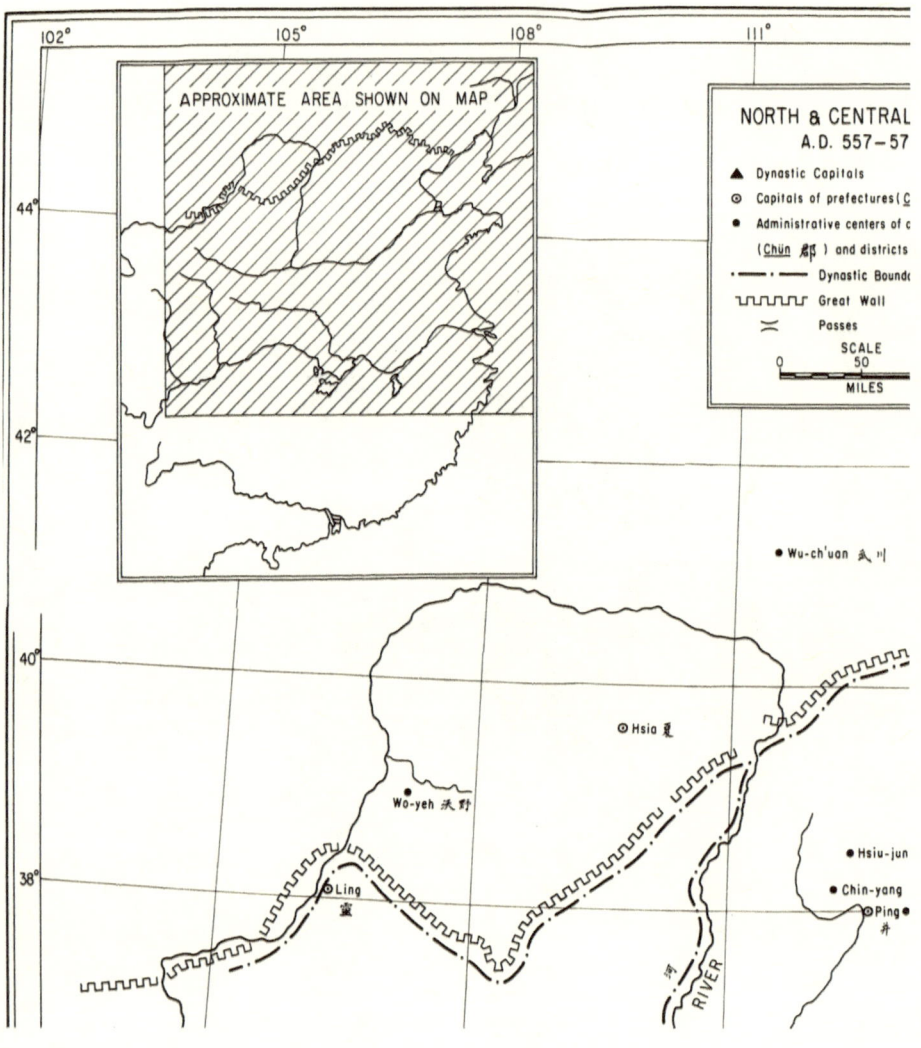

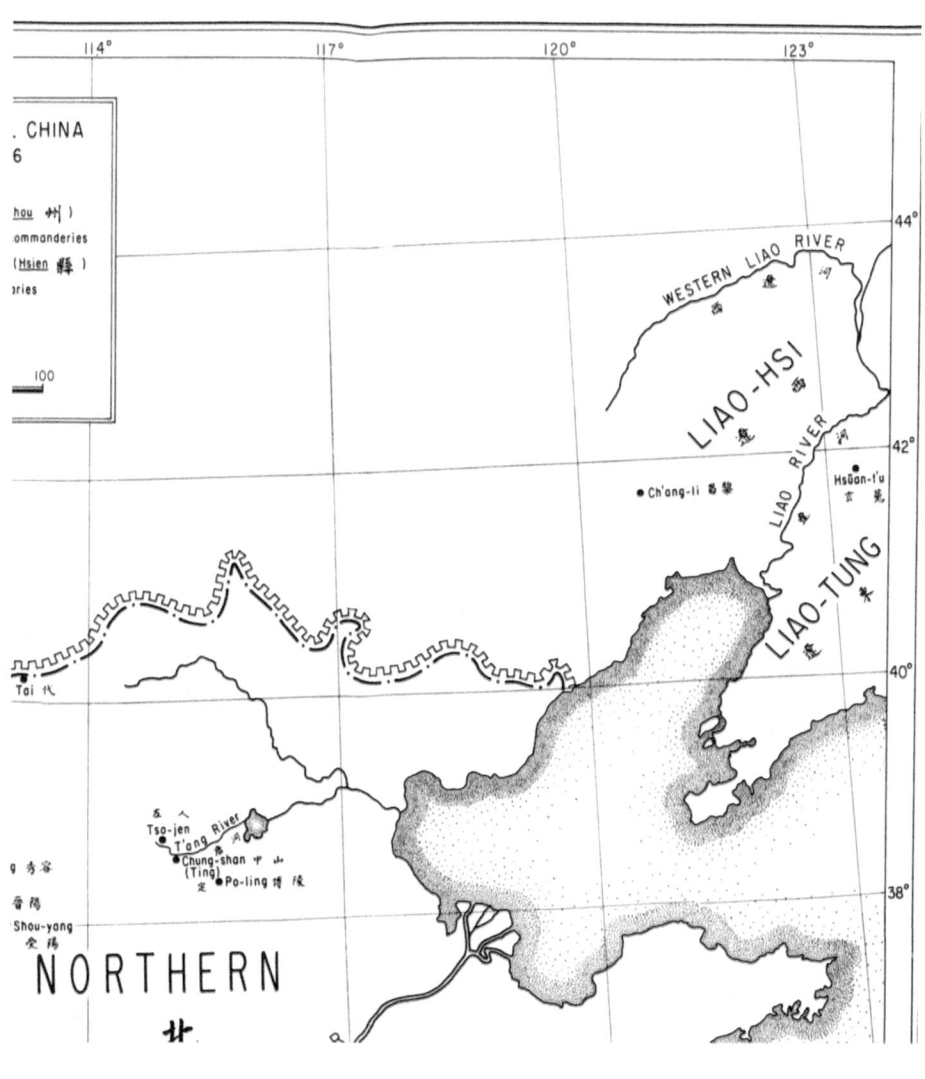

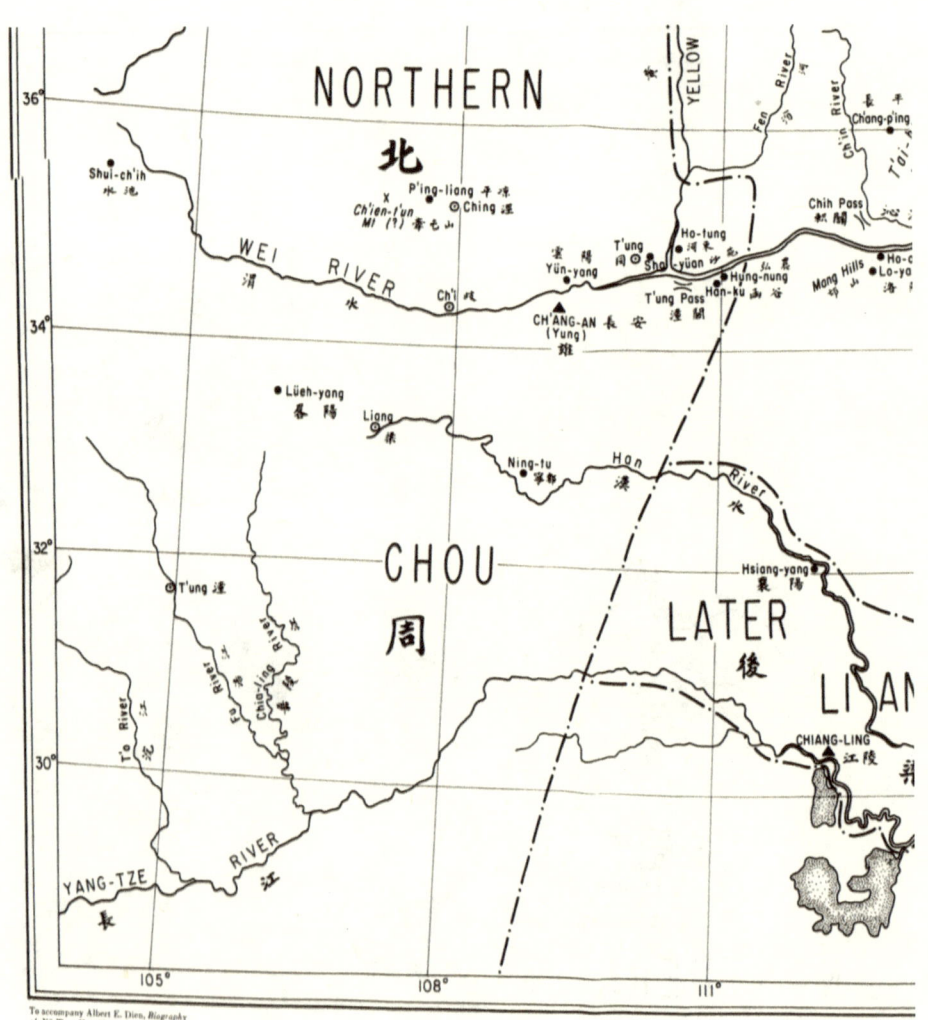

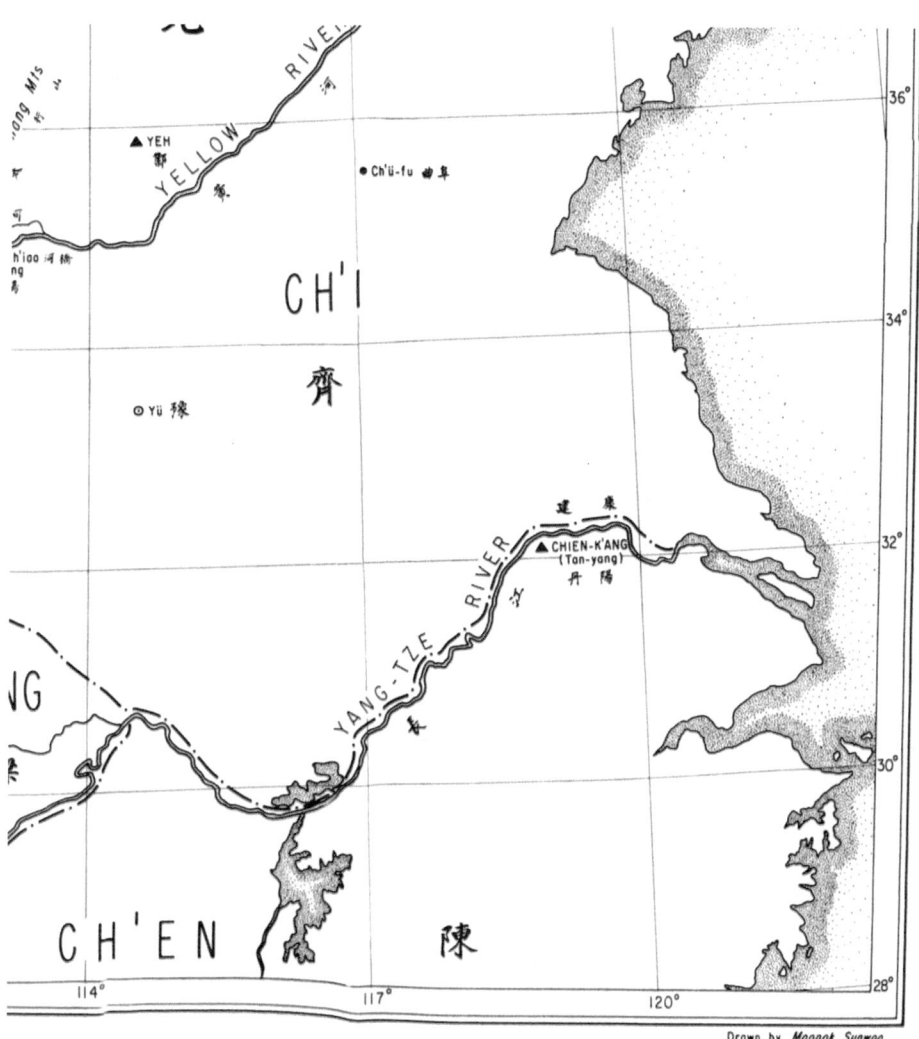

www.ingramcontent.com/pod-product-compliance
Lightning Source LLC
Chambersburg PA
CBHW021710230426
43668CB00008B/784